TONGUES of ANGELS UNVEILED

Mysteries of Speaking In Tongues Unlocked

Musa George Mwanza

BOOKS BY MUSA GEORGE MWANZA

Tongues of Angels Unveiled

God's Medicine Bottle for Sin and Addictions

BOOK COMING SOON

Kingly and Priestly Authority

Unless otherwise indicated, all the scripture quotations in this volume are from the King James Version of the Bible.

The other translations used in this edition:

NKJV	New King James Version
BBE	Bible in Basic English
MKJV	Modern King James version
NIV	New International Version
AMP	Amplified Bible
DBY	Derby's Translation
WEB	World English Bible

TONGUES of ANGELS UNVEILED...Mysteries of speaking in tongues unlocked.

Musa George Mwanza
P.O BOX 1015
Jeffrey's Bay
6330
South Africa.

E-mail: musagmwanza@gmail.com

ISBN 978-0-620-54708-6

Cover design: The Office 4 u - Jeffrey's Bay South Africa.

DEDICATION

I would like to dedicate this book first and foremost to the God of Israel, the Lord and father of our Lord Jesus Christ. Who allowed me to receive all the insights and revelations in this book. To my wife, Hope, who is the love of my life, my best friend and ministry partner. I look forward to discovering all the mysteries of the Holy Spirit with you. To our children who are our great joy, Mariska and Joash. May you continue to grow in the ways of the Father as you grow in age.

To the Christ Ambassadors, my beloved team through whom the Lord opened this realm of operation in me. I love you guys. To brother Shadreck and the Leadership team of Christ Ambassadors Outreach Team.

To Pastor George Kambika, a dear friend and partner in ministry and to all our ministry friends who are breaking the barriers of knowledge to enter into the deeper realms of glory.

Lastly but not least, to all our partners and intercessors with whom we credit the amazing favour of opening the gates of supernatural wisdom to the church and to the world.

ACKNOWLEDGEMENTS

My upmost thanks go to my dear Holy Spirit of God, for the gift of tongues and for further expounding the mystery of tongues to me. To my wife Hope, for her most valuable support of prayer and understanding. To brother Shadreck for your contribution towards the book and to the ambassadors for the articles on tongues, and to my fellow 2009 LXP students for the testimonies.

To Papa Floyd McClung Jr, for the foreword and words of encouragement. To my brother and friend Pastor George Mwanza for being there for my family. For always taking care of our physical and spiritual needs.

Finally, to my wider LXP family for their moral and spiritual support.

CONTENTS

FORE WORD

When God stirs a person to long for His empowering presence, that person can only respond one of two ways. They can open their heart to God, or grow sceptical towards the Holy Spirit. Far better to be passionate and learn wisdom, than to grieve the Spirit through cold-heartedness!

This book is biblical, passionate, and wise. It is written by a godly man who longs for the power of the Holy Spirit. It is thorough and practical, based on firsthand experience. I highly recommend it to you!

I bless you dear brother, and I pray your book will be a blessing to many, many people!

Yours,

Floyd McClung Jr.
International Director, All Nations Family.

INTRODUCTION

The subject of tongues is one subject that has been on my heart for quite some time now. I have had a long journey with the Lord on this subject. Now, I am very excited to share what the Lord has revealed to me and has had me experience concerning this subject. Last year in the year 2010, I asked my students at Christ Ambassadors Outreach Team to share with me in writing what they understood on the subject of speaking in tongues. Here are some of the views my students expressed about the importance of speaking in tongues:

"He that believeth and is baptised shall be saved, but he that believeth not shall be damned. And these signs shall follow them that believe in my name shall they cast out devils; they shall speak with new tongues." (Mark 16:16-17).

"Because we believed, were saved and baptized, these signs mentioned in the above scripture shall follow us. This is because we believed. It is as simple as that.

Praying in tongues is a sign that we belong to God's family. It also makes us one in Spirit with God as we pray in tongues. It causes us to speak directly to God because no one is able to hear what we are speaking apart from Him to whom we are praying. Praying in tongues also brings about God's presence and encourages Spiritual gifts in our lives such as the gift of prophecy.

Above all speaking in tongues can build you up and give you boldness. It also causes you to speak mysteries which can be your revelations for the day or year."

- Kelias Phiri -

8

Introduction

"First of all, tongues are a sign for the unbelievers. The Bible says the gift of speaking in tongues in strange tongues is proof for unbelievers and not for believers. I believe that in every kingdom there is a language that people use to communicate deep and secret matters. When someone is born again, he /she is born into a kingdom called the Kingdom of God. In this Kingdom, the language we speak to communicate secret things directly to God is tongues.

Speaking in tongues is not optional in this kingdom because it is a sign that you belong to this Kingdom. Every believer has to speak in tongues; a believer cannot effectively grow in the things of the Spirit without speaking in tongues. The Bible makes it clear in (Jude 20) that in order to build yourself up in the Most Holy Faith you have to pray in the Spirit. Praying in the Spirit simply means praying in tongues. Apostle Paul said he who speaks in a tongue edifies himself. In other words, he who speaks in a spiritual tongue builds and strengthens himself. Therefore, the importance of speaking in tongues is that it makes believers grow.

The second thing is that tongues helps believers to speak with God directly. 1 Corinthians 14:2 says, *'For anyone who speaks in a tongue does not speak to man but to God for indeed no one understands him. He utters mysteries to God.'* A person who speaks in tongues speaks not to man, for he utters mysteries to God in a mysterious language.

What are these mysteries? Mysteries are things that are beyond human understanding. Mysteries are secrets. A believer who speaks in tongues speaks secrets to God

such that no one can understand what he is saying."
- Isaac Epignosis Tembo -

"Tongues are Holy Ghost given (Acts 2:1-2). Many people today ignore tongues. They don't know the power of tongues in their lives. In 1 Corinthians 14:2 we have heard that he who speaks in tongues does not speak to men but to God, for no one understands what he speaks. However, in the Spirit he speaks mysteries.
Tongues can build your inner man (1 Corinthians 14:4) and your faith (Jude 20).

Another thing that tongues can do is that they can correct your past. This is because spiritual tongues are eternal. They are not limited by the realm of time. For example, if you have curses running in your bloodline, in tongues you can uproot and destroy the root of the problems rather than just the effects and symptoms. Tongues are able to activate your spirit to be sensitive to the reality of the heavenlies. They are also able to transform the logos Word of God into a Rhema Word; a Word filled with life and authority. Tongues also have the ability to draw you closer to God and make your spiritual antennas to be sensitive and actively receiving signals from the Spirit.

Tongues can make you healthy in your body, handsome and beautiful, and brighten every area of your life. They can change things in the Spirit for your benefit, and activate your mind to the things of God. Speaking in tongues also kills the flesh in you.

The more you speak in tongues the more you grow your spirit man and the more the flesh degrades."
- Emmanuel Zoe Mwansa -

Introduction

"Tongues are a language of the Kingdom. The Bible says that for those who believe, these signs shall follow them; they shall force out demons, if they drink any deadly thing it shall do them no harm. We need to understand that above all, tongues are a sign to show that someone is a believer of Christ and has been baptised in the Holy Ghost. Therefore, it is not a matter of choice or preference, but it is a spiritual law that whosoever believes should speak in tongues.

The Bible says that he who speaks in tongues does not speak to men but speaks unto God. This is because no one can understand the things he is saying. Speaking in tongues is one of the ways which helps us grow in the things of God because it prepares our hearts for the receiving of the Word of God. Tongues helps the Word of God to be deeply rooted and grounded in our hearts. Tongues activates our spirits to the things of the Spirit. It brings edification to our inner man. The Bible says what should I do? When I pray, I will pray with my Spirit and also with my understanding. Then I will sing with my Spirit and also with understanding.

There is not any other way of praying with the Spirit other than speaking in tongues. When stressed and tired, we should pray in tongues because it has the ability to refresh and to give us rest.

The Bible says when we speak in tongues we speak mysteries. These mysteries when revealed become revelations and insights into the Spirit. As we speak in tongues our spirit, through the Holy Ghost, searches the deeper things of God.

I thank God that I do speak in tongues and that the deep things of God are open to me!! Glory to God!"
- Canaan Sophia Sakala -

As shown from the different understandings of the mysteries of tongues among some of the Ambassadors, tongues have a much deeper significance than what many have believed. Understanding the mysteries of tongues is a key to functioning in the deeper wisdom of God.

In the pages of the chapters of this book, we shall go through a stage-by-stage study of the mysteries of tongues. This edition will prepare you for a life of supernatural wisdom as we journey together to unveil the deep and hidden things of the Spirit of God.

Part 1

Discovering Tongues

And they were all filled with the Holy Ghost, and began to speak with other tongues, as the Spirit gave them utterance.

$$\boxed{1}$$

Why Pray?

Ever since I was born again in the year 1997, I had always wanted to make sense of the mystery of God's dealings with humankind. This desire to know more about God's dealings and about His involvements in running the affairs of this world caused me to pursue several prominent men and women of God for answers. This quest for understanding was usually left unsatisfied as these ministers of God simply claimed that God was in control of all the affairs of this world.

As I watched the news seeing everything happening in the world, I became more and more distraught at the constant devastation and destruction. I would often wonder how the God who calls Himself love could allow all the wars, hatred, crime, and injustices. Does He not see all the innocent children dying of hunger, the number of orphans mushrooming, and the astronomical number of marriages breaking apart? How could God allow such madness? Isn't He supposed to stop all this? Isn't the God of peace supposed to bring peace?

Many people, young and old, who are victims of the injustices and the evil of this world, do not understand how the God of peace continually allows all the evil happenings in this world to perpetuate, share these questions with me. In my experience with working among young people, I have discovered that this ideology of God being in control of all the affairs of this world is drawing young people away from Christ.

This often happens when young people lose their parents through death or tragedy, or experience other such evils and injustices in their lives. After such trauma, they resolutely blame God for allowing their parents to die which therefore subjects their lives to many hardships. They feel rejected and abandoned by this alleged God of love. These young people have fallen into the belief professed by many teachers and preachers that God has done or allowed these things to happen to them. I have counselled many people who are disappointed and angry with God for the loss or death of their loved ones. Many have asked me, "How can you tell me God loves me when He took away my parents?" Many continue to blame God for their circumstances and end up being eaten away by bitterness and unforgiveness throughout their lives. They grow up as both physical and spiritual orphans as day by day, their hearts grow colder and harder towards the Lord. They are left never knowing the Father heart of God, nor of the depths of His healing love for them. Their lives are completely stolen from them as a result of these erroneously false teachings and misconceptions of God's truth.

I continued to experience more and more confusion on this thorny issue as I found myself having to counsel people and explain to them why they should trust God again after He has allowed their loved ones to die so prematurely. How can you trust someone again after he has so grievously violated that trust?

I really sought the Lord for answers until I came upon a statement in a book by Andrew Knowles called Discovering Prayer. The statement, *"It seems God cannot do anything for humanity unless somebody prays."* This became so profound to me because it appeared to answer one of my greatest questions about God's involvement in this world. As I continued to study on this matter, I discovered that God does not run affairs in this world. His good and perfect will is not always being done in this world except in the lives of those born again and fully surrendered to Him and to His will. Hence, the Lord Jesus prayed, *"Let your will be done on earth as it is in heaven."* (Matthew 6:10) He would not have admonished us to ask for the will of God to be done on earth if the will of God had already controlled all the affairs of this world. How I look forward to the time when His will is fully accomplished throughout the earth!

This concept is easier to understand when you grasp the meaning of **2 Peter 3:9MKJV** which states:

> *"The Lord is not slow concerning His promise, as some count it slowness, but is long suffering towards us NOT WILLING THAT ANY OF US SHOULD PERISH, but that ALL OF US SHOULD COME TO REPENTANCE."*

If God's will is that no one should perish but that all should come to repentance, then it is clear that His will is not always being done on the earth. People perish every day without knowing Jesus as their Saviour. The scripture also states that the Lord is patient (long-suffering) concerning His promise to come back to this world to redeem the church because He wants everyone to receive salvation before His great and dreadful day.

When individuals accept Jesus Christ as their personal Lord and Saviour, the will of God begins to carry out in their lives through the process of yielding to the Word of God and to the heeding of the Holy Spirit. If God's will really was in total control of the world today, then all people would have received salvation because His will is for all to come to salvation. If His will was fully accomplished, then peace would have reigned throughout the earth and true love among all people would be evident. Righteousness and justice would have been the order of the day instead of the torrid reign of their opposites. It would be normal for all the attributes of God to be seen and expressed throughout the world. The will of God for this world is summed up in Revelations 21:4 which declares, *"And God shall wipe away all tears from their eyes; and there shall be no more death, neither sorrow, nor crying, neither shall there be any more pain: for the former things are passed away."*

It was only then that I finally discovered that the creator of this world is not running affairs in the world! After such a mighty discovery, other questions arose in my heart. Why is this so? How can God create the world and not fully run it His way? Why is it that evil seams to prevail in the world created by the God of righteousness?

In answer to my questions, the Lord took me to
Genesis 1:26:

> *"And God said, Let us make man in our
> own Image, after our likeness. And Let
> them have DOMINION over the fish of
> the sea, and over the fowl of the heavens
> and over cattle, and over ALL THE
> EARTH, and over all the creepers
> creeping on the earth."*

Then He took me to **Genesis chapter 9:2** which
confirms that He is not running the affairs of this world.

> *"And the fear of you (Man) and the dread of
> you shall be upon the animals of the earth
> and upon every bird of the air, upon all that
> moves on the earth, and upon the fish of the
> sea. Into your HANDS they are
> DELIVERED."*

Psalms 8:6 further summarizes this:

> *"You made him (man) rule over the works
> of the hands; you have put all things under
> his feet."*

These three scriptures reveal that from the beginning
God did not have dominion over the earth. He did not
say to Adam, "I will **DOMINATE** through you." He
actually gave man the authority over all of His creation.
Everything He created was put under man's dominion.
Genesis 9 confirms the dominion that was given to man
when God declared that all creation would have a fear of
man. The fear referred to is a reverence kind of fear, one

that respects God's hierarchy of creation. It is not the intense holy version of the fear that God the Father expects from man. God gave us the same place of dominion on earth as He has in heaven. Therefore, the responsibility to run affairs on earth from the beginning of time was given to man. Since man was in perfect fellowship with God before sin entered the world, the will of man was in perfect alignment with the will of God.

Perfect Fellowship

God and man lived in perfect fellowship before the fall. This means that man, his wife, and God were in one accord and of one mind. In fact, all creation was in harmony with God and man as man was placed in authority over it and assigned all creatures their names (Genesis 2:20). The earth actually bore vegetation and fruit in abundance without the toil of man until sin entered and brought a curse unto creation (Genesis 3:17-19).

Interestingly, Adam and his wife, Eve, were naked yet bore no shame before God or each other because shame did not yet exist on the earth. It was sin that brought the awareness of shame or guilt to man and drove a wedge in between the direct intimacy of God and man. The perfect fellowship between man and God was broken as a result of sin and they became aware of their nakedness **(Genesis 3)**. This rift was evident when they hid for the first time from God when they heard Him coming towards them (verse 10).

The Breakaway of Man from God's Fellowship

Suddenly sin appeared between the best of friends and all the trust and confidence disappeared from man's side. Man had fallen from this perfect fellowship and forfeited the glory that once covered him as the ruler of the earth.

Job in chapter 31:33 puts it clear when he said that Adam actually covered his transgressions, he tried to hide his sin from God.

> *"If I have covered my transgressions as Adam, by hiding my iniquity in my bosom."*
> **(Job 31: 33 NKJV).**

Both Adam and Eve failed to take ownership of their sin before God. They did not acknowledge their mistakes, nor did they hold themselves accountable for their own actions. Both blamed someone else for their wrongdoing. Adam blamed his wife and his wife blamed the serpent. This introduced a complete disregard for the individual responsibility of one's actions. God, however, made the consequences of sin and disobedience clear to all. It brought curses, pain and suffering, separation from God, and ultimately death **(Genesis 3)**.

This fall of man from the perfect fellowship with God brought a different kind of rule into this world. Adam was deceived into giving the dominion he had been given by God to the devil. From that day forward, the devil became "the god of this world," (2 Corinthians 4:4) by his taking the authority and dominion that God had originally given to Adam in the beginning of creation. He, therefore, is the one who runs the affairs of this world; the injustices, the wars, the suffering, sickness, and death. His rule will run until the lease of Adam runs out and Christ rules the world. The lease of Adam will run until the life in the flesh is over, especially for believers until glorification.

The whole world is under the power of the evil one. The devil is the one running the affairs of this world. The systems, the ways, and all the works of this world are under his authority. The authority he stole from Adam is now in his hands.

The extent of his dominion is shown in the book of **Romans 8:20-22**, which states:

> *"For the creation was subjected to vanity, not of its own will, but because of him who subjected it, in hope ,that the creation itself also will be delivered from the bondage of decay into the liberty of the glory of the children of God. For we know that the whole creation groans and travails in pain together until now. "*

The whole of creation fell subject under the power of the evil one against God's original plan. The scripture above shows that the whole of creation is in bondage of decay, corruption, and death. It groans and travails in pain with hopes of one day going back into the original place under the authority and Lordship of the Sons God.

The Word that God gave to Adam that the creation will have fear of you is still in operation, but in the hands of the god of this world. God cannot go against his

Word. His gifts are without repentance. So the authority and dominion that was originally meant for Adam is in the hands of the evil one until the lease of Adam ends (Adam is the same word as man, the lease of Adam therefore means the time that man was given to rule over all creation see Daniel 7:9-14; revelations 20:4; 2 Peter 3:13).

God does not have fellowship with satan and therefore does not influence the affairs of this world unless someone who has fellowship with Him asks Him in prayer. God directly intervenes in the running of the affairs of this world when someone prays and asks Him. God is able to bring forth His plans and purposes through the lives of those who are in tune with His heart and are filled with the Spirit.

> *"Therefore I exhort first of all that supplications, prayers, intercessions and giving of thanks be made for all men, for kings and all who are in authority, that we may lead a quiet and peaceable life in all godliness and reverence. For this is good and acceptable in the sight of God our saviour, who desires all men to be saved and to come to the knowledge of his truth."*
> **(1Timothy 2:1-4 NKJV).**

The above scripture admonishes us to pray for all men, for kings and those in authority for the will of God to prevail in this world. We need to pray for peace to prevail in our families, towns, cities and nations and for the Rulers and Kings of this world to rule with justice and righteousness. This is a good and acceptable practice before the Lord. He fervently desires to stop the works of the evil one in this world.

The Spirit through Apostle Paul, admonishes us to pray many kinds of prayers for the will of God to take effect on earth. Even His desire to see everyone come to the saving knowledge of our Lord Jesus will happen when we pray. Prayer brings the will of God back into this world. It is powerful. It is effective. (James 5:16) It changes what takes place in the earth. It affects whose will is accomplished and whose is not. It is therefore the believer's responsibility to call upon the Lord, to declare His promises, His truths, and His will in the power of His name in every circumstance.

2

What is "Praying in the Spirit?"

"Praying always with all prayer and supplication in the Spirit, and watching thereunto with all perseverance and supplication for all saints..."

(Ephesians 6:18).

Growing up in a non-Pentecostal church gave me a lot of confusion with the issue of praying in the Spirit. There were many unsatisfactory explanations as to what "praying in the Spirit" really meant.

During these early years of my Christian life, I believed praying in the Spirit was simply praying vigorously with a loud voice or putting up a solemn face during worship. Then, in 2003 my best friend who was also a leader with me at church, suddenly began speaking in other tongues. This rattled my theology a bit because I had learnt from many preachers that tongues was a gift of the Spirit and that not everyone can be gifted in the same way. With this understanding, I was divided between the earnest desire to be baptised in the Holy Ghost and to speak in other tongues and the belief that tongues was just a gift that God could choose not to give me.

The desire was so strong that it translated into seeking God for understanding of this mystery. After about two weeks of praying and seeking, I attended a conference at one of the local churches called Grace Ministries. On the last day of the conference, the man of God prayed for me and I was baptised in the Holy Spirit with the evidence of speaking in other tongues. What an amazing and revelatory experience that was! It was then that I truly realized that praying in other tongues was not just for a selected few but also available for every believer in Christ.

From that day on, I have spoken in my prayer language frequently and have made it a part of my daily prayer life. As I attended more Spirit filled meetings, studied more of the Word of life and prayed more in tongues, I even experienced marked changes in my tongue "vocabulary."

Interestingly, I was not a typical candidate for speaking in tongues from a church denominational perspective. I was not a Pentecostal. I grew up in a traditional conservative church where the things of the Spirit were not only not taught but were also a taboo subject. I was still in the traditional church when my friend and I received the baptism of the Holy Ghost. From the time that I was baptised in the Holy Spirit, I have fervently preached that tongues are for the whole body of Christ. Seeing many people I have prayed for also receive their spiritual languages has given further credence to this understanding that the gift of tongues is available to all. Furthermore, I have even seen some rather unlikely, often cynical candidates who were baptised in the Holy Spirit and are now undeniably "tongue talkers."

Up until today, however, I still face the same significant question of what praying in the Spirit really means. It is a great subject of debate within the body of Christ. Many still believe that praying in the Spirit requires either a solemn face and quiet contemplation or quite the opposite of jumping around screaming loudly and expressively while praying. From the opening scripture in the book of Ephesians 6:18, the apostle Paul admonished us to *"pray in the Spirit."* What did he mean when he said this? I deduced that if Paul wrote to the Church at Ephesus and admonished them to pray in the Spirit, then whenever he spoke about praying in the Spirit, he would mean the same thing.

Paul further elaborated that, *"He who prays in tongues, does not pray to men but to God, for no one understands him, however, in the Spirit he prays mysteries."* (1st **Corinthians 14:2**). Evaluating the above scripture makes it significant in that it directly relates speaking in other tongues to praying in the Spirit. Therefore, if speaking in other tongues meant praying in the Spirit in first Corinthians 14:2, then Paul meant the same in Ephesians 6:18 in the opening scripture. Another scripture in Acts confirms this truth in an account by a different apostle.

This scriptural passage talks about the events of the day of Pentecost when the Spirit descended from on high as follows:

"And they were all filled with the Holy Ghost and began to speak with other tongues; as the SPIRIT GAVE THEM UTTERANCE... "
(Acts 2: 4).

Now let us read in Darby's Translation the same passage of scripture:

"And they were all filled with the Holy Spirit, and began to speak with other tongues as the SPIRIT GAVE TO THEM TO SPEAK FORTH. " **(Acts 2:4 DBY).**

Praying in the Spirit is praying with the utterance of the Spirit of God. The Spirit will give you a language, which the scripture in **(1 Corinthians 13:1)** describes as the language of the angels. When praying in the Spirit we communicate things, which are beyond the scope of the human mind and the earthly realm. From the passages of scripture above, it is evident that there is a language *of* the Spirit used when praying *in* the Spirit.

Now I will quote from the **Amplified Bible** to get a different perspective and obtain more clarity to this truth.

"For if I pray in an (unknown) tongue, my spirit (by the Holy Spirit within me) prays, but my mind is unproductive-bears no fruit and helps nobody (unfruitful). Then what am I to do? I will pray with my spirit-by the Holy Spirit that is within me; but I will also pray (intelligently) -

> *with my mind and understanding; I will sing*
> *with my spirit-by the Holy Spirit that is within*
> *me; but I will also sing (intelligently) with my*
> *mind and understanding also.*"
> **(1 Corinthians 14:14-15).**

See this same passage also in the **Bible in Basic English** Translation:

> *"For if I make use of tongues in my prayers,*
> *my spirit makes the prayer, but not my mind.*
> *What then? Let my prayer be from the spirit,*
> *and equally from the mind; let my song be*
> *from the spirit, and equally from mind.*"
> **(1 Corinthians 14:14-15).**

Apostle Paul declared, *"I will pray with my spirit···I will pray with my understanding."* This shows that praying in the Spirit must have an element of not having understanding with your mind. Tongues that are beyond man's natural and mental understanding satisfy this element of not having understanding with the carnal mind. On the other hand, he said that praying in understanding has everything to do with the mind, meaning those things that the mind can interpret. From my experiences, I discovered that praying in the Spirit is not limited to speaking in other tongues. I experienced a kind of praying where words failed to come out of my mouth. I would speak words from my spirit but the words would seem too big to come through my mouth. This usually left me slain on the floor.

This often happens when tongues or any other words are not potent enough to express the deep longing of your spirit. This happens to me usually during my private prayer time. The other kind of praying in the Spirit which I have experienced is "groaning" in the Spirit during prayer. This kind of tongue comes mainly during intercession.

Therefore, if speaking in other tongues is not for the body of Christ today, then we cannot pray in the Spirit as the body of Christ. We are spirit beings and so cannot afford to neglect praying in the Spirit. We are called to a spiritual kingdom. In order to function more effectively in this kingdom we need to use the spiritual language. Praying in the Spirit according to scripture is therefore, praying in tongues!

3

What is "Praying in Understanding?"

Since the day, I was born again, "praying" had always meant, "praying in understanding." (Praying in words, I understood, using my mind and my intellect). I, like many other believers, believed that the only sure way to pray was in complete understanding. Praying in understanding, therefore, meant that I knew exactly what I was praying. Since I knew exactly what I had wanted to pray, I thought that I had to speak in words I understood to the Father. Besides, I knew that praying in other tongues was a controversial topic which I should steer clear from. Even after being baptised in the Holy Spirit with the evidence of speaking in other tongues, I still was confused about the matter of praying in tongues because I was not praying in the understanding of my mind.

I was afraid and confused, especially when I first started praying in tongues, because now I just spent a little time praying in human understanding and most of the time praying in tongues. This was different for me because I wanted to be like every other believer around me who would pray for a long time in understanding before they would start speaking in other tongues.

Once again, I found myself digging into the Word of God and praying for more understanding and clarity on this matter.

This pursuit took me to the Lord's Prayer **(Matthew 6:9-10 NKJV):**

> *"In this MANNER therefore pray: Our Father in heaven, Hollowed be your name. Your kingdom come. Your will be done on earth as it is in heaven. "*

The idea of the disciples asking the Lord Jesus to teach them how to pray seemed very strange to me. This is because in the Jewish culture, people start learning from the Torah very early in life. Moreover, praying must obviously be one of the first things they would learn to do as children.

With this in mind, I believe there must have been something fundamentally different about the way the Lord Jesus prayed that made the disciples want to know how to pray *His way*. Prayer would have been given a fundamentally different meaning in the way the Lord Jesus prayed. The disciples evidently sensed its power and authority in a much different way than they had ever known before. Jesus did not merely recite memorized verses from the Torah. He prayed with personal intimacy with the Father and with authority. They also wanted to know how to do this. This is why the disciples asked Him to teach them how to pray.

What is "Praying in Understanding?"

By the teaching of the Spirit, I understood the wording the Lord Jesus used to come up with the meaning of this prayer. *"He said in this MANNER, which also means in this WAY, or in this FASHION, pray."*

The Lord Jesus showed us the way to pray. He said "you should pray in this manner." He gave us the guidelines on how to pray in this fundamentally new way that the Heavenly Father desired of us. In this new way of praying, He firstly acknowledged the existence of God in heaven and then glorified Him by acknowledging His Holiness. Then He taught us to ask for the Kingdom of God (by the Holy Spirit) to come-. At this time, the Lord Jesus was the only one who had the kingdom in Him through the Spirit of God.

> *"But if I cast out the demons BY THE SPIRIT of God, then the KINGDOM of God is come upon you."*
> **(Mathew 12:28 NKJV).**

> *"For the Kingdom of God is not eating and drinking, but righteousness and peace and joy in the HOLY SPIRIT."*
> **(Romans 14:17 NKJV).**

In this way, the Lord Jesus was telling us to ask God the Father for the Holy Spirit, so that at the fullness of time we could worship the Father in Spirit and in Truth. He then prayed *"Your **WILL** be done on earth as it is in heaven."* This was so profound because the Lord Jesus was admonishing us to pray in line with the Word of God. According to **(Romans 12:2),** the will of God is in the Word of God. The Lord Jesus gave us a framework of how to pray in understanding and ask for the Holy Spirit because He understood that the Spirit of truth would lead us in all truth and teach us how to pray in the Spirit.

The manner, in which the Lord Jesus showed us to pray to the father in understanding, was firstly to acknowledge His Holiness and His Name. Then to ask for the Kingdom to come, which is actually asking the Holy Ghost to come. *"For the kingdom of God is not meat and drink; but righteousness, and peace, and joy in the HOLY GHOST. "* **(Romans 14:17)**. At this level, I discovered that praying in understanding is not as simple as it is usually perceived to be. As I went through the scriptures, I found that according to **(Job 38: 2),** one can withdraw the light of the plans of God through his or her prayers. *"Who is this that darkens my counsel with words without knowledge? "* I realized that this can be a very serious matter and an offense to God as one can actually defeat and deplete God's will through praying unintelligibly. Praying in the Spirit always prays forth God's will. Praying with our understanding may not. In the Spirit, I will not pray my fears, nor my will, but God's.

Scripture declares that God's beloved people perish due to lack of knowledge. Many people, like Job, go to God with complaints about their circumstances, and disturb the holy countenance of God with their complaints. They withdraw the light of God while they are thinking that they are praying. God responds to faith and not to emotions and complaints. Complaining words are dead words, hopeless words, and faithless words.

What is "Praying in Understanding?"

These words reject God's presence and truth from the situation.

For this reason, there is little or no talk about this kind of praying. The devil knows that the church is already deceived in this area. He sees that many in the church pray their circumstances and their will, their way, and not God's Word. The Lord only responds to His Word; He is always looking for His Word in every prayer we make in order to perform it.

> *"Then the Lord said to me, ̒you have seen well: for I keep watch over my word to give effect to it.̓*
>
> **(Jeremiah 1:12 BBE).**

> *"Then the LORD said to me, ̒you have seen well, for I am READY to perform my word.̓*
> **(Jeremiah 1:12 NKJV).**

The Word **"ready"** comes from a Hebrew word **"SHAQAD,"** which means, **"sleeplessly being on the lookout."** The Lord is therefore on the **"lookout"** day and night to perform His Word. The Words of Our Lord Jesus in (John 15:7 KJV) confirm this truth as shown below;

> *"If you abide in Me, and my WORDS abide in you, ye shall ASK (pray) what you desire, and it shall be done for you.̓*
> **(John 15:7 NKJV).**

The Lord only responds to His Word, because He and His Word are one *"...and the Word was with God, and the Word was God."* (John 1:1).

Prayer from the Soul

The Scripture makes it clear that the power of death and life is in the tongue; likewise, our prayers can bring death or life. Prayers also originate from the heart and come through the tongue. *"Out of the abundance of the heart, the mouth speaks."* *(Matthew12:34)* Likewise, prayers that originate from the soul of a person produce negative results in a way that can impose curses upon us. This can be a thorny issue among Christians, but James wrote to and about Christians when he warned about this issue in **(James 3: 14-15 NKJV);**

> *"But if you have bitter envy and self-seeking in your hearts, do not boast and lie against the truth. This wisdom does not descend from above, but is earthly, sensual, and demonic."*

The word **"sensual"** comes from Greek word, which means **soulish.** The word **"earthly"** likewise comes from a word, which means *flesh*, which is the unrenewed mind. At the fall of Man, his spirit was cut off from God and as a result, the soul and the flesh began expressing themselves independently. This made the flesh to start lusting for its own pleasures in opposition to the spirit. This produced the lusts of the flesh, which Scripture describes as the fruits of the flesh, like envy, jealousy, self-seeking, etc. Therefore, people who still live by the flesh, pray the fruits of the flesh to the people they pray for and even unto themselves.

What is "Praying in Understanding?"

You may pray all the right words but the dominant message is what is in your heart. It is not so much about the prayer made, but about the hearts and lives of the prayer; are we liars, prideful, self-seeking, gossipers? Oftentimes, people may look like Christians, involved in many church activities, but in reality, their rebellious attitudes and conduct can grieve the Holy Spirit of God and cause offence to the body of Christ. It once happened to me, during one of my weekly prayer meetings. The person leading the meeting instructed us to pair up in groups of two and pray for one another. I was paired with a brother who prayed self-pity over me. This brother brought his assumptive troubles that I supposedly face in ministry. He complained to the Lord on my behalf as if I told him I was struggling in those areas.

I felt worse after the prayer than before, I felt like something dropped into my spirit that made me feel heavy laden and discouraged. For the first time, I had thoughts of self-pity. I felt the pressure of being a husband in missions. I worried about my child's future and further provision for me and my family. I began to miss the job I had before coming to South Africa. This went on for days until the Spirit revealed to me that I had allowed the spirit of self-pity to come upon me through the prayer and laying on of hands. Upon this realisation, I had to repent, pray, and rebuke the spirit of self-pity to get it out of my system and out of my thought life.

Since that moment, I learned not to allow just anybody to lay hands on me or even just to pray for me. There is actually a transfer of spirit that takes place through the laying on of hands. Just as the Holy Spirit can be conferred, so also can other spirits be transferred to someone else **(Acts 8:17)**. While much good can be accomplished through such prayer, I must emphasize that one should also use discernment. While many people assume that all prayer is always acceptable to God and its effects are always beneficial, this is actually not equivocally true. If we do not submit ourselves to the Holy Spirit and seek His direction, then even our well-intentioned prayer may be motivated by fleshly attitudes and a wrong spirit. I do not want someone involved in witchcraft, immorality, or rebellion to lay their hands on me any more than I want someone with depression, fear, or a critical spirit. Ever notice how being around positive, happy people makes you positive and happy? Ever notice the same effect when you are in the company of very negative, critical complainers? Furthermore, I also do not want someone to pray their will over me and my situations rather than the Lord's. The Holy Spirit will not endorse prayers that come from such attitudes nor with wrong spirits, nor will He present them before God the Father.

Inevitably, our praying degenerates into the pattern we have seen in James 3:15: This is earthly--------- soulish---------demonic. The effect of such prayer is like soulish talk, negative or positive. It releases against those for whom we are praying an invisible and indefinable pressure, which does not relieve their burdens but rather adds to them. Some people may pray for you whose prayers you would be better off without. That may sound shocking, but some people have their own ideas of what other people's ministry should be or how their problems should be fixed. They may try to pray their own agenda into being but it may not be the will of God at all. You may experience confusion and pressure against you every time you try to do certain things that they are praying against.

There is hardly such a thing as prayer that is not effective. The question is not whether our prayers are effective. The question is whether their effect is positive or negative. Their effect is determined by the power and spirit that works through them. Are they really from the Holy Spirit? Or are they a soulish counterfeit? The power of soulish prayer is both real and dangerous. The result it produces is not a blessing but a curse.

How to Pray in Understanding

The Lord has given us all things that pertain to the fullness of life and Godliness. Therefore, when we pray, we should always know, that whatever we could ask for in prayer He has already given unto us. We should declare what He has done for us, His Word, His promises and truth. We should acknowledge what He has given us, through the life, death and resurrection of our Lord Jesus.

Our prayer in understanding must always be born from faith in accordance with His Word. We should not focus on the circumstances but on what the Lord in His Word has said. We should always pray in accordance with the Word of God. For you to effectively pray in understanding you have to keep the Word of God in your heart. In the book of **(John 4),** the Lord Jesus admonished us to pray in Spirit and in TRUTH. The only way to pray in truth is to pray in line with the truth, which is His Word.

One needs revelation of the truth to effectively pray in understanding. You have to have understanding of the will of God. You must be in tune with the Holy Ghost for you to function effectively in prayer in understanding. This is when the order of praying becomes very important in SPIRIT and in TRUTH. Praying in Spirit will make you in tune with the Spirit. This will set you up for effective prayer in understanding as you pray in alignment with the will of God, in tune with the Spirit. The Spirit leads us into all truth.

In his book, *The Seven Spirits of God*, Pastor Chris Oyakhilome shares the following example of how to pray in understanding:

"Father, in the Name of the Lord Jesus, I understand from the Word of God that you'll take charge of my circumstances if I let you. You are the Lord of my life, and I pray that you order my steps today in the course that you've already planned for me. I want to meet only the people that you plan for me to meet today, and hear, and say the things you plan for me to say.

I function as a child of God today in the anointing of the Holy Spirit. I walk in your light, in the Name of the Lord Jesus. There's nobody coming into my world as an accident today. The Spirit of dominance is at work in me today, in the Name of the Lord Jesus.

I refuse to fear, for though I walk through the valley of the shadow of death, I fear no evil, for You are with me; Your rod and Your staff comfort me. I refuse to be defeated today, for I am a victor in Christ Jesus. I'm more than a conqueror, in the Name of the Lord Jesus.

What is "Praying in Understanding?"

Thank you Lord for Your presence is with me today. I thank You for the Spirit of excellence is at work in me. I do not act foolishly or utter foolish words. The wisdom of God is found in my month, and I give counsel by the Spirit today. I deal with people by the Spirit today. I see with the eyes of God today, in the Name of the Lord Jesus Christ.

Oh Lord God, I thank You, because good things are coming my way today. I receive in the Name of the Lord Jesus. And I'm a giver today; I'm a blesser today, in the Name of the Lord Jesus. My body is yielded to You, every fibre of my being and every bone of my body is for the Holy Spirit. I'm Your living tabernacle today. Talk through me; move through me; walk through me; talk in me, in the Name of the Lord Jesus.

The health of God is in me. I refuse to let my body be subject to sickness, disease and infirmity. Every fibre of my being is inundated by the life of God. I'm walking in divine health, in the Name of the Lord Jesus. Glory to God!"

You can also pray in understanding for your family members and colleagues as shared by Pastor Chris Oyakhilome in the Seven Spirits of God:

"I thank You Father for my children. The anointing is upon me and them. They can't but do the will of God. They can't but work the works of God. They can't but live in the Word of God, in the Name of Jesus. No devil hatched in hell can touch them. I thank You Father, For Wisdom is in the mouth of my wife and in her heart.

She functions in the things of God today, in the Name of Jesus.

I pray for every one of my staff in the Name of Jesus. They cannot but do the will of God and think the thoughts of God. In their going out and in their coming in, not one of them is subject to the devil. The Word of God is in their hearts and in their mouths in the Name of the Lord Jesus!"

You can add anything to this kind of prayer but always know that we pray the promises of God over our lives and the lives of our friends and family. Amen!

┌─────────┐
│   4   │
└─────────┘

Who should "Pray in the Spirit?"

$\mathcal{M}$any different ideologies have been born from this one question. It has caused extreme division in the Body of Christ for centuries and never ceases to give rise to heated discussions. Some believers hold the stance that praying in the Spirit was only available for the apostles of the early Church. This means that there should be no contemporary "tongue talkers." Others, such as Pentecostals, hold views that praying in the Spirit or in other tongues is available to all. Still others argue that individuals should not pray in tongues publicly unless there is interpretation. These confusions and arguments about praying in the Spirit are conceived by the devil. He wants to make the Body of Christ impotent as it neglects such a powerful potential weapon in their arsenal against him. He always seeks to get our focus off that which imbues us with the conquering power of God and precisely what God wants accomplished on the earth. He loves to steal our

43

attention off of the things of God and onto division which perpetually weakens the Church. Theological debate over who in the Church is right and who is wrong is a favourite strategy of the enemy. How better to get people not to pray in the Spirit than by convincing them that it is not for them? Meanwhile, believers neglect other important assignments, which nourish and expand the Kingdom of God on earth.

The devil has attacked many believers in the body of Christ with dullness of perception so that they do not understand the truth in the Scriptures.

The Lord Jesus referred to this matter after His resurrection in the book of Luke, as shown below:

"Then He said to them, "O foolish ones, and slow of heart to believe in all that the prophets have spoken. "
(Luke 24:25 NKJV).

The same plague of dullness of mind was also present in some of the disciples of our Lord Jesus. All the disciples were told about the coming death and resurrection of Jesus Christ. However, when the Lord Jesus was resurrected, some of the disciples could not believe the things that He had taught them earlier. *"It was Mary Magdalene, and Joanna, and Mary the mother of James, and other women that were with them, which told these things unto the apostles. And their words seemed to them as idle tales, and they believed them not. " (Luke 24:10-11).*

Who should "Pray in the Spirit?"

The disciples took the words of the women who brought the good news of the resurrection our Lord as foolish stories, idle tales.

Unfortunately, this mentality is still prevalent in the lives of many believers of today. They read the Word, they hear the sermons, but to them these words are idle and inactive. They do not see the kinetic, living power these words contain. They do not realize the tangible force of life contained within these scriptures.

Has your perception of God's Word become dull? Does it seem stale and inapplicable to your life? Do you want to understand the mysteries spoken by the apostles and prophets of old? Ask Jesus to open the eyes of your heart and give you understanding of His truth.

> *"And He opened their understanding, that they might comprehend the scriptures."*
> **(Luke 24:45 NKJV).**

From the above scripture we can see that, the Lord Jesus opened their eyes of understanding so that they could comprehend what the scriptures were saying. Likewise, believers of today can also have their eyes of understanding opened in order to fully understand the scriptures.

No one can understand the truths of the scripture unless the Spirit opens their eyes of understanding to see the truth. For us to perceive the truth we need the Holy Spirit to give us the ability. Apostle Paul's prayer for wisdom for the Body of Christ in Ephesus should be every believer's daily prayer. If you want to have your eyes of understanding opened to the truths in God's Word, pray this with me:

"That the God of our Lord Jesus Christ, the Father of glory, may give to you the Spirit of Wisdom and revelation in the knowledge of Him; The eyes of your understanding being enlightened; that you may know what is the hope of his calling, what the riches of his glory of his inheritance in the saints. And what is the exceeding greatness of his power towards us who believe, according to the working of his power. "

(Ephesians 1:17-19(NKJV).

The secret to living a victorious life is in understanding the hope of your calling, your inheritance in Christ and the working of His power (who is the Holy Spirit). When your eyes are opened to understand the mysteries of God, you will function very effectively in your new life as a believer. This prayer is not only for the ministers in the five-fold; it is for EVERY believer in the body of Christ. If you did not know, now you know that every believer in the body of Christ is called to understand the hope of their calling and the working of the Holy Spirit. Every believer has to have knowledge of the extent of Christ's calling in his or her life.

Who then should pray in the Spirit? Is it for a specific kind of person? Is it for the whole body of Christ? Let us examine what apostle Simon Peter said when he preached the Word of truth to the people in Jerusalem:

Who should "Pray in the Spirit?"

"Then Peter said unto to them, repent, and be baptized EVERY ONE OF YOU in the name of Jesus Christ for the remission of sins, and you shall RECEIVE THE GIFT OF THE HOLY SPIRIT."

(Acts 2:38).

These highlighted words should give us a clue as to what kind of people should pray in the Spirit. Apostle Peter admonished everyone to repent and be baptised, and then to receive the gift of the Holy Spirit. He was preaching the message of hope to ordinary men and women, saying ecumenically that if they repented, they could also receive the gift of the Holy Spirit. From the above scripture, it is evident that the gift of the Holy Spirit is available to all believers so that all can function and pray in the Spirit.

The Words of Jesus confirm this truth as recorded in the gospel according to Mark (Mark 16:17). The Lord Jesus commanded His disciples to preach the gospel to every creature and said something very profound about who should pray in the Spirit.

"And these signs shall follow then that BELIEVE; in my name shall they cast out devils; they shall SPEAK with NEW TONGUES."

(Mark 16:17).

In the above scripture, the Lord Jesus declared that the signs above should follow men and women who believed the truth of the gospel from His disciples. The Master meant us, the people who received and believed the gospel from the apostles. Praying in the Spirit is therefore a sign that one is a believer according to the Lord Jesus. Every believer can actually be baptised in the Holy Ghost at the time he/ she is born again with the evidence of speaking in tongues. As it was in the account of Acts 2, after receiving the Word of grace and accepting the Lord Jesus as their Lord and saviour, they were baptised and spoke in tongues at that very moment. However, due to dulled minds, many in the body of Christ believe that praying in the Spirit is only for mature Christians. I also believed this lie for most of my early Christian life until I got the revelation of the scripture above. It was so liberating that I went on to test it to see if it were really true.

One evening I was teaching at one of the Christ Ambassadors Outreach Team's meeting. I called for an alter call and six guys responded to give their lives to Christ. After leading them to Christ, I laid hands on them and prayed for their baptism in the Holy Spirit. Immediately they were baptised in the Holy Spirit and started to speak in other tongues. This was so profound to me and to the ambassadors. This wonder brought a new lease of life to the team as a new revelation yielded results. More of the same happened in our meetings as more and more of the ambassadors were baptised in the Holy Spirit. This news went out so quickly that I started receiving people from other ministries who were born again for some time to be baptised in the Spirit.

I recall one particular incidence when a girl named Rebecca, from the Bible Gospel Church heard about what was happening at our meetings. She came to attend one of our meetings. On that particular day after I finished teaching, I asked if anyone needed prayer. This girl just whispered to me saying, *"I wish I could speak in other tongues."* It was then that I told her she absolutely could! She then responded by saying, *"I hope so."* So I said to her,

"With God, you don't wish and hope, you just believe and you will receive!"

She then said, *"I believe!"*

After she said this, I asked her to come to the front. I held her hands and under the unction of the Holy Spirit blew on her, and said to receive the Holy Spirit. She immediately fell under the power of the Holy Spirit, praying in tongues and praising God.

Another incidence was of three old women in their sixties from the Reformed Church in Zambia. I taught them that the gift of tongues was for the whole body of Christ. These people come from the very church I was expelled from for speaking in tongues. In a nutshell, I prayed for these women and immediately they were all baptised in the Spirit with the evidence of speaking in tongues.

From that moment on, I truly believed that praying in the Spirit was not only for a select few, but equally available to every believer in Christ. Since then, many people came and received the baptism of the Holy Spirit with the evidence of speaking in tongues from our ministry. Therefore, if praying in the Spirit is for all the believers in the Body of Christ, why then is it that many believers still do not pray in the Spirit?

I think that one of the main reasons that many believers still do not pray in the Spirit is because they simply do not believe that praying in the Spirit is available to the entire body of Christ. This is especially true among non-Pentecostals. Due to this belief, many do not desire more of the Spirit. The scripture declares that God will grant us the desires of our hearts. We need to have a desire in our hearts for the greater things of the Spirit for God to give them to us. Therefore, if we desire of the Spirit, He will give us the gifts of the Spirit. However, if we do not desire more of what He has for us, He will not give it to us. Apostle Paul admonished us to desire Spiritual gifts as shown below:

> *"Pursue love and **DESIRE SPIRITUAL GIFTS…**"*
> **(1 Corinthians 14:1 NKJV).**

You will not receive what you do not desire and you will not desire what you do not believe!

On the other hand, many Pentecostals believe in praying in the Spirit, but only for the ministers of the gospel and the mature in Christ. Many among the Pentecostals still fall into the same category as Rebecca did. Those are the ones who just wished they could speak in other tongues but did not actually expect to receive it for themselves. The kingdom principles are established in believing and expecting. God's kingdom principles are not founded on the tenets of wishing and hoping. Those who believe and act in faith on what they believe will see the glory of God in their lives through the manifestation of the Holy Spirit. The Lord Jesus said this very well when He answered Martha, the sister of Lazarus:

> *"Did I not say to you that if you would **BELIEVE** you would see the glory of God?"*
> **(John11: 40 NKJV).**

Another group of believers among Pentecostals claim to have believed for this gift of the Spirit yet did not receive it. They often say, *"I have been prayed for more than once."* And that, *"I believed to receive the gift of tongues each time that I was prayed for, but I still was not baptised.* **Thinking** that you believe and **actually** believing are two very different things. To believe is to perceive and understand the reality behind the mystery in faith. In this case, to believe is to perceive and to understand that tongues are your inheritance for you in the NOW.

> **All things are possible if only you believe!**
> *Jesus said to him, "If you can believe, all things are possible to him who believes."*
> **(Mark 9:23 WEB).**

There are also believers who simply cannot yield to the Holy Spirit. They are often trying to help the Spirit along by erecting a certain religious posture or being overly emotional when praying. These religious acts do not amount to believing. Emotions are wrought from the senses of the mind and can frequently distract us rather than direct us to believe. These attempts can only succeed to harden our hearts so that we do not yield to the Holy Spirit. Be sober, be real, be yourself. Then the Spirit will take over your spirit and you will be baptised in the Holy Ghost. Learn from the Lord Himself when He spoke through the Psalmist:

> *"Be still and know that I am God; ⋯"*
> **(Psalms 46:10 NKJV).**

The words *"Be still"* comes from a Hebrew word **"RAPHAH"** . Raphah means among other things *"to cease, to leave, to forsake and to let along."* Therefore to be still is to cease trying, to fully allow the Spirit do His work in you without your trying to help Him. You have to let go, yield to whatever He wants to do, and allow Him to work. I must emphasize that I am not meaning to bring any condemnation on those believers who have yet to receive their prayer language. What I do want to do is to bring liberation so that all believers can grab hold of this special gift of the Spirit for themselves.

In addition, the word used for *"know"* in the above scripture comes from the Hebrew word **"YADA."** Yada has the meaning of "giving the whole being, having intimate knowing as a husband knows his wife." Having that element of being vulnerable, being naked before the Father, positions you to receive from Him. Just give your whole being to the Lord and stop trying to help Him. Do not even try to imitate others. Just let go and let the Spirit do His work His way!

Inevitably, there will always be sceptics seeking to disprove someone else for whatever reasons they can find. While it is essential to always use discernment as to what is of God and what is not, weighing things of the Spirit by the scales of the mind will often result in confusion, cynicism, and unbelief. Faith, by definition, is not logical. It is *"being sure of what you hope for, certain of what you do not see."* *(Hebrews 11:1)* It is understood with your heart and not your intellect. The natural mind cannot understand the things of the Spirit. The natural mind cannot access the things of the Spirit.

Who should "Pray in the Spirit?"

People who are, earthly and worldly in their minds cannot receive things of the Spirit. Get out of your box; allow the Word of God to become wisdom to your heart. It is only then that you will make sense of the things of the Spirit.

The Gift of the Spirit is for you

Apostle Peter declared at Pentecost that "the gift of the Holy Spirit" was for you and for your children and for all who are far off, even as many as the Lord our God shall call. **(Acts 2: 33-39).** This is the same gift which came with the ability to pray in the Spirit (speaking in tongues). It is for you who have been called into salvation. The gift is yours to grab by faith!

Similarly Apostle Paul in **1 Corinthians 14: 39-40,** while warning the church at Corinth that "all things must be done properly and in an orderly manner," further expressed his wishes that those to whom he wrote all spoke in tongues by adding that they "do not forbid speaking in tongues." The gift of tongues is for everyone who is saved and believes. Leap out in faith and grab your inheritance in Jesus' name!

5

Why Pray in Tongues?

One day I was praying with my spiritual brothers at church. Then one brother uttered a statement that brought me into deep contemplation. He said, *"We need to pray hard because if the devil defeats the head, then the whole church will be defeated."* This statement posed some poignant questions to me during and after prayer. This is because I know that Christ is the head of the Church and that the devil cannot defeat the church. *"And I say also unto thee, that thou art Peter, and upon this rock I will build my church; and the gates of hell shall not prevail against it."* (Matthew 16:18) Then I realized that there actually are some ministries that are defeated by the devil. Ministries that are dead spiritually by being overcome by sin and wickedness and that no longer bear fruit. Upon seeing this, I asked myself, "How can a ministry be defeated if the Church cannot be defeated? How can the devil defeat a ministry in an already victorious church?"

Then the Lord revealed to me that the devil can cause defeat to a ministry by causing confusion in the Church regarding its heart and lifeline in the Holy Spirit. The devil skilfully uses confusion to deprive many believers from understanding the greater mysteries of the Holy Spirit and giving Him access to their lives. This, consequently, causes a sense of spiritual atrophy and death in some of the believers in the body of Christ as it stymies their ministries.

*"**For as the body without the Spirit is dead,** so faith without works is dead also. "*
(James 2:26 NKJV).

The above scripture declares that, as the body without the Spirit is dead, so the body of Christ without the Spirit is dead. The Holy Spirit is the life of the Church. He is the source of revelation, counsel, and power. He is the one who gives life to the Word of God. This is the reason why the Lord Jesus asked His disciples to wait in Jerusalem until they are endued with life power from on high.

This life power is the Holy Ghost. Without the Holy Ghost there would be no Church as we know it today. Hence, Jesus' clear command to wait until they received what He knew was essential for the Church to grow and thrive.

"And, behold, I send the promise of my Father upon you: but tarry ye in the city of Jerusalem, until ye be endued with power from on high."
(Luke 24:49).

The Church is the witness of Christ; we witness the reality of Christ in our lives and to those around us. With this understanding, we learn from the below scripture that the presence of the Holy Spirit in the Church is what makes the Church alive. The Spirit gives the Church life to exist as the body of Christ and not just as a club of religious people.

> *"But ye shall receive power, after that the Holy Ghost is come upon you: and ye shall be witnesses unto me both in Jerusalem, and in all Judaea, and in Samaria, and unto the uttermost part of the earth.*"
>
> **(Acts 1:8).**

The Parable of the Body

The Lord in teaching me further on the subject of the body of Christ gave me a parable. Firstly, He started by asking me two very important questions about the body. The questions were:

"How does the body function?"

"What are the two deciding organs of the body?"

Now I know that the heart and brain are the two deciding organs of the body. I immediately thought that if the brain is in the head, then what exactly does it control? The brain controls, among other things, the functions of the body including eyesight and hearing. The heart, on the other hand, is the custodian of life itself as it pumps the lifeblood throughout the body. It is responsible for the core issues of life. The heart digests the thoughts of the head and gives them life. The heart is

56

the master of the will and emotions; it determines how your day, even how your year will be.

The Lord then explained to me that a person with brain damage or with an underdeveloped brain can live, but a person with severe heart damage or deformity usually dies. This is because the life of every person is in the heart. The body of Christ, much like a human body, needs a healthy brain and heart to live life to the full. Therefore, if a person exercises the brain through academic exercise, his/her brain will grow and function more efficiently. Likewise, if a person does physical exercise and eats healthily, his/her heart becomes healthy, efficient, and strong.

The head of the Church is Christ who is the living Word of God and the heart of the Church is the Holy Spirit who is the resurrection power and the life. This means the body of Christ needs the Word of God, who is Christ, the head, to see and to hear, to perceive and to understand what God is doing. The brain controls these abilities from the head who is Christ the living Word.

Hence, this means that if the body of Christ wants to interact more with God through the spiritual senses of seeing, hearing and speaking, the body needs proper sustenance. It must continually feed the head with the healthy food of the Word and exercise it through studying and meditating on the Word. Likewise, the body of Christ needs the Holy Spirit who is the heart and the custodian of life to have life. Without the Holy Spirit, the body of Christ has no life just as without the heart, the human body has no life.

The Holy Spirit gives life to the Word of God. He manifests the Word of God the same way the heart interprets thoughts into actions. The same manner of which we do physical exercise for strengthening the heart, we need to do spiritual exercise to strengthen the heart of the Spirit. A vital way of exercising the heart of the Spirit is through speaking in other tongues, or praying in the Spirit.

> *"For bodily exercise profits a little, but godliness is profitable for all things of the life that now is and that which is to come."*
> **(1 Timothy 4:8 NKJV).**

Praying in other tongues presents the body of Christ with the ability to strengthen its inner man. It emboldens and empowers the Church, enabling it to participate in and activate the will of the Father in the earth.

> *"That He would grant you, according to the riches of His glory, to be strengthened with MIGHT in the inner man, that Christ may dwell in your hearts through faith; that you being rooted and grounded in love, may be able to comprehend with all saints what is the width and length and depth and height to know the love of Christ which passes knowledge; that you may be filled with all the fullness of God."*
> **(Ephesians 3:16-19 NKJV).**

The word **"mighty"** as used in the above scripture comes from a Greek word **"DUNAMIS."** This word dunamis means miraculous power. It also means miraculous ability. This, therefore, infers that speaking in tongues gives the body of Christ the power and ability to grow in the love of God as they spread forth His message of truth. Speaking in tongues makes the Body stronger, mightier as it is further rooted in love. This gives forth the ability to ascertain what the width, and length, depth and height of the love of Christ profoundly entails.

Speaking in tongues also gives the ability to release the love of God deposited in our hearts by the Holy Spirit. Tongues activate and edify the gifts of the Holy Spirit in our lives. They also have the ability to grow the seed of love poured into our hearts directly by the Holy Spirit. **(Romans 5:5)**.

Tongues have the ability to strengthen our spiritual selves and to deepen our intimacy with the Father. Praying in tongues also gives us the ability to enter into the place of our inheritance here on earth as God by His Spirit, causes us to participate in His divine will, nature, and purpose.

Commanding Angels to do Business For Us

Another significant reason why we need to pray in tongues is that it enables us to communicate certain coded truths which instruct angels to do business on our behalf. Apostle Paul in 1 Corinthians 13 calls tongues the "language of angels." Paul also admonishes us that we shall in fact judge angels. He understood that as we speak in other tongues we instruct angels to bring our inheritance, fight our battles, and take hold of our possessions on our behalf. This truth is shown in the book of Hebrews.

"But to which of the angels said he at any time, Sit on my right hand, until I make thine enemies thy footstool? Are they not all ministering spirits, sent forth to minister for them who shall be heirs of salvation?"

(Hebrews 1:13-14).

The Lord sends his angels to minister to us in every way we ask as we speak in other tongues.

One man of God told an interesting story of his life experience when he went through some physical challenges with his health. He prayed to the Lord who showed him through a vision that he was bound by the power of witchcraft. After this startling revelation, he immediately commanded the chains of witchcraft to break in the name of Jesus, but nothing seemed to happen. However, when he prayed in other tongues, the power of darkness loosed him and the sickness left him at once.

I believe when the man of God prayed in other tongues, he commanded angels to set him free from the hold of the enemy and it was done.

Another situation also happened during my preparation for a trip to South Africa. I was with my wife getting together what we needed to go to the South African High Commission for our visa applications when the chequebook went missing. We had to draw some money for the visas so this was not the time for our chequebook to disappear. We looked for the chequebook everywhere but still could not find it. Then I said to my wife to stop looking, just go ahead and prepare breakfast, and the chequebook would find itself. We had our breakfast and did everything else we needed to do to get ready. Then I went to our bedroom mirror and said, *"I charge you (cheque book) by the power of the Holy Spirit to show up! I command the angel in charge of me to bring it forth in Jesus' Name!"* From the mirror, I moved as if I was pulled straight to where the chequebook was. My wife is still amazed at what happened that morning. Glory be to God!

I believe the angel responsible for me took me by the hand to show me where the chequebook was. It was an awesome experience to know just how much the angels of the Lord are dedicated to serving us.

Another incidence happened to my wife, Hope. She had unfortunately dropped her cellular phone in the water and it immediately stopped working. I remember after coming from work, she had immediately told me of the whole ordeal. I felt charged in my spirit and asked her to give the phone to me. I held the phone in both hands and spoke in tongues for a short while. When I said amen, the phone was working. It is amazing what praying in tongues can do to the glory of God!

Praying in Tongues Gives Rest

Praying in the Spirit or speaking in tongues gives rest. This is the kind of rest written about in Hebrews chapter 4. This rest only occurs when the Word mixes with faith. Praying in other tongues, gives the inner man the ability to mix the Word with faith so that we can enter into God's rest. Isaiah explains it:

There is a rest found in speaking in tongues. It is a refreshing feeling of deep rest that can be only compared to a sound and peaceful sleep. A few years ago in Lesotho during an outreach, I spent a lot of time with the Lord praying in tongues on a nearby mountain. One morning when I came down from the mountain for the meeting, one of my group leaders asked me whether or not I was sleeping. He had noticed that I looked inexplicably well rested and refreshed simply from being in the presence of the Lord. During my days in college when I was pursuing my chartered accountancy, I, without realizing the whole concept, used to pray in tongues each time I got tired of studying. It worked so well that just after about 30minutes of praying, I would feel refreshed and rejuvenated to go for more hours in my studies.

The general peace and rest of God comes from the harmony between our spirit and the Spirit of God. Each time you feel burn out with work, studies, or any kind of stressful situation or task, just have communion with the Spirit through praying or singing in the Spirit. Praying and singing in tongues brings refreshment and can completely revive us in a short period of time.

Praying in Tongues Builds a Spiritual Giant in You

My pastor would say there was a time for physical giants, like Goliath in the days of King Saul. There is a time for mental giants like Isaac Newton or Albert Einstein who both revolutionised modern science. "Now, is the time," he would declare, "when God is raising spiritual giants who will understand the very mysteries of the heavenlies and help to usher in great moves of the Spirit never seen before."

Spiritual giants can come from all different walks of life. There is not one common look or background from which they emerge. However, one thing they do all share is an understanding of their position in Christ. They are a people who can withstand the wiles of the enemy after the enemy has done all to make them fall. They are not prideful, people pleasers in constant fear of what others may think about them. Spiritual giants are mysterious people; they are a special kind of fruit of God's creation. They are a people who understand their authority in Christ and know how to use it. These people are bold as a lion, but loving and meek like the Master who has encapsulated their hearts.

There is a frequently quoted passage of scripture in the book of Ephesians that I believe is greatly misunderstood in the body of Christ today. It contains keys to becoming Spiritual giants that many seem to miss. The famous scriptures are **Ephesians 6: 10, 11 and 18:**

>*"Finally, my brethren be STRONG IN THE LORD and in the POWER OF HIS MIGHT."* **(10)**

>*"Put on the whole armor of God that you may be able to stand against the wiles of the devil."* **(11)**

>*"Praying always with all supplication IN THE SPIRIT..."* **(18)**

The apostle Paul admonished the Body of Christ in Ephesus, firstly to be *"strong in the Lord,"* which means to be strong in the Word of God. The Lord is the Word, which manifested into flesh and lived among us **(John 1:14)**. If you search the scripture in Acts 20: 32; you will discover that the Word of God is able to build you up into the inheritance that was prepared for you by the Father. By implication, we can say that Apostle Paul challenged the church to be strong in the Word, by saying be *"strong in the Lord."* The other key highlight is, *"in the power of his might,"* which is the Spirit of God, His dear Holy Spirit. Implied in Paul's exhortation was the challenge to the Church to be *"strong in the Spirit."* By speaking more in other tongues, you strengthen yourself in the Lord. *"He who speaks in a (strange) tongue edifies and improves himself..."* *(1 Corinthians 14:4 AMP).*

This is what it means to put on the whole armour of God, *to be strong in the knowledge of His Word and in the power of Holy Spirit*. The secret to being strong *"in the power of His might"* is in spending time praying in the Spirit or in other tongues. Sometimes the Lord will even fill you to the point of drunkenness in the Spirit to imbibe you with the strength of the power from on high that you will need.

Paul concludes by saying to pray ALWAYS with all supplications in the Spirit. He admonishes us to pray always in tongues in order to strengthen our inner man with mighty power so that we can be effective for the Gospel.

"But you beloved, building up yourselves on your most holy faith praying in the Holy Spirit."
(Jude 1:20 NKJV).

There are two striking points I want you to note in the scripture above. The first is the phrase, *"building up yourselves,"* which is translated from a Greek word **"EPOIKODOMEO"** which means to build upon. This does not refer to building in terms of construction from scratch. Rather, it means building a structure on an already existing foundation. The Bible tells us that God has dealt a measure of faith to every man **(Romans 12:3)**. Each one of us was given a measure of faith as a foundation for our lives. It is on this foundation that we need to build a superstructure of faith upon. In essence, the faith given to you by God is the foundation you need to build a supernatural life. It leads to the health, success and victory required for us to become giants in the Spirit. The second point from this scripture I want to emphasize is the term **"most holy faith."** This refers to your highest level of faith. Faith, therefore, is experienced at different levels. Sometimes, while under the influence of God's Word, your faith can be so stirred up that at such moments, you are inspired to take supernatural steps you normally would not. You become energized to speak God's Word with power and do great exploits for Him. Such high moments of spiritual intensity and soaring levels of faith is what the Bible refers to as "your most holy faith." Your most holy faith is the highest level your faith has attained at any given time. The Lord is saying to you to build up a superstructure on that highest level of faith. Never let your faith fluctuate like the waxing and waning phases of the moon. Let your highest level of faith become your new benchmark of belief from which to launch.

According to Paul, praying in other tongues is the way to access greater levels of faith. As one who is born again, you have already been given a measure of faith. However, faith is initially given to you in seed form, and that little measure must grow if you want to grow in the Lord. You must develop your faith to its highest level. This is why praying in other tongues is such an INDISPENSABLE spiritual activity for every believer. Keep growing your faith through the Word **(Romans 10:17)** and build up yourself on your most holy faith by praying in the Holy Ghost. Praying in the Spirit has the ability to grow your Christian life in ways you can never achieve by natural means.

6

Tongues and Gifts of Tongues

"And these signs shall follow them that believe; In my name shall they cast out devils; they shall speak with new tongues."
(Mark 16:17).

They shall speak with new tongues, they who believe in the in the Name of the Lord Jesus (Mark 16:17). Speaking with new tongues is one of the signs that shall follow them that believe. Casting out devils is another sign of a believer.

A tongue is a supernatural language available to every believer, primarily as a sign of evidence of being baptised in the Spirit. Tongues are also referred to as the language of the Spirit. Therefore speaking in other tongues is also an effective sign of the presence of the Holy Spirit in our lives. Every believer who has the Spirit of God in him or her can speak or pray in other tongues. Speaking tongues is evidence of the presence of the Holy Spirit in a believer's life for the Spirit prays from within him. The Spirit gives the ability and the language of tongues as He dwells in our lives. As shown in the scripture below:

"And they were all filled with the Holy Ghost, and began to speak with other tongues, as the spirit gave them utterance."
(Acts 2:4).

The entrance of the Holy Spirit into your life brings eternity in you and gives you a special language or utterance called tongues. Tongues spoken of in the opening scripture are double-edged words. To unbelievers, tongues are a sign distinguishing these followers of Christ from all others. To believers, they confirm that we are of Christ and that His Spirit dwells within us. They show a people not of this world yet in this world to bring God's kingdom power to earth. Unbelievers can never fully understand believers because they lack the spiritual understanding of God's reality. Tongues, therefore, will be difficult for unbelievers to comprehend since it is a gift of the Spirit. To those without faith, it is foolishness. To those who know God, tongues are a vital instrument for spiritual growth. Tongues automatically taps us into the realms of the Spirit.

"Therefore tongues are for a sign, not to those who believe but to unbelievers..."
(1 Corinthians 14: 22 NKJV).

Every believer is a new creation with a new heart and a new Spirit (not of stone but of flesh, Ezekiel 36:26), new life because you are dead to sin but alive unto Christ (Colossians 3:3), with a new nature (not of sin but of righteousness 2 Corinthians 5:17-21), and also a new tongue to pray in Spirit and in Truth (1 Corinthians 14:2). Every believer must therefore, be able pray in tongues because it is in your new nature, as a believer. You are not of this world but of heaven and tongues are your heavenly languages.

Gifts of Tongues

There is a tongue dialect for every believer to speak. It is different and unique to every believer just as one's relationship with God is unique. It may contain many words or a few simple sounds. All instantly enable you to tap into the spirit realm and make intercession for your situation, even in areas unbeknownst to you. Tongues confirm the presence of the Holy Spirit in the believer's life. It is a must for every believer to speak in his/her tongue! God designed it specifically as a spiritual tool given to help His children to grow in their spiritual walk with Him.

There is also another kind of tongue that is not for personal edification. This kind of tongue is given at a singular moment for the purposes of ministering publically to the growth and edification of the Church. These words are always followed by interpretation and often yield a timely prophetic insight or special exhortation from the heart of God. They may be of a completely different spiritual language than that individual's normal prayer tongue as it is a separate gift of purpose. These kinds of tongues are given as gifts by the Holy Spirit to anyone He wills to fulfil certain ministry needs and reveal that which He is doing.

"There are diversities of gifts, but the same Spirit. "
(1 Corinthians 12:4 NKJV).

"...to another different kinds of tongues; to another Interpretation of tongues."
(1 Corinthians 12:10 NKJV).

These kinds of tongues are given to certain individuals to operate in for specific functions. These tongues are not for someone to operate in all the time, they are given by the Holy Spirit to specific individuals to operate in for the purposes of fulfilling certain specific functions and meeting certain specific needs. These tongues manifest in different ways for the purposes of meeting and perform different kinds of needs and activities. These tongues manifest as four different kinds. These are:

1. **Tongues of Prophecy**
2. **Tongues of Intercession**
3. **Tongues of Praising and Magnifying**
4. **Tongues in Familiar Languages**

The Holy Spirit can often give an individual a special gift of prophecy in order to prophesy to the Church even when that is normally not their main gifting. The Spirit is not limited in how He accomplishes His purposes or in whom He uses to speak when He has willing and yielded vessels. For example, I am called first to teach the oracles of God. Prophecy is not my primary role in the body of Christ. However, I have found myself prophesying more and more frequently as the Holy Spirit finds need. When the Spirit of the Lord is present, He distributes gifts to individuals who are available to fulfil certain of His desires. The same thing happens with faith; the scriptures declare that every believer is given a measure of faith **(Romans 12:3)**. The Spirit also gives the gift of special faith for individuals to operate. Christians operate at a certain faith level for every level of growth attained. This level of faith is what is proportionate with our growth.

There are times when our level of faith is insufficient for a particular need. At this place, the Holy Spirit gifts with a gift of special faith for purposes of fulfilling His will. This is not usually your normal level of operation in faith. Laying hands on a dead man's body lying in a coffin and commanding him to be raised to life requires a stronger, bolder faith than does praying for a tummy ache to cease. The Spirit may choose to gives you this great faith to use for the sake of the people He wants to heal, to deliver and to save. This often happens with anointed preachers and evangelists who operate in gifts of healing and especially, recreative miracles. God increases faith to unleash His desired miracles before us in ways we normally would not be bold enough to perform. It just shows all the more that it is He who performs the miracles for His glory. We are simply the vessels He chooses to use.

We can also say the same about gifts of tongues. The Spirit of God gives gifts of diverse tongues to fulfil certain needs and desires. He can give you a tongue of specific intercession if there is a life and death situation. He can give you a tongue of prophecy and interpretation if He wants to deliver a specific message to the church.

He can also give you a tongue in a familiar vernacular if He wants you to minister to a people with a foreign language. He can even give a tongue of praise and magnification if He wants to have quality fellowship with you in your ministering to Him.

7

Different "Kinds" of Tongues

𝒯his topic had been one of the most troubling as I was growing in my early Christian life in a Reformed Church. Many times I was put on trial by the elders of the church because of this very matter. Their argument was if I could speak in other tongues then I had to interpret what I was saying in my prayers to the church. It was very difficult for me to explain because even I could not understand the things I was saying. They judged me on this point, and eventually, sadly, they asked me to leave the church based on this very issue. This was a very difficult time for me as I was actively involved as a youth leader and a teacher for the youth at that same congregation. However, it was used strategically by the Lord to launch me into deeper pursuits in Him.

After leaving this church, the same one I grew up in, I went to a Pentecostal church right there in Lusaka. My time at this new church was very exciting because I could pray without anyone spying and reporting on me. I could speak in tongues freely and did not have to feel so guarded or limited in the things of the Spirit. This went on for some time as a kind of incubatory period. I was growing in my walk with the father day after day. However, there was one thing that really bothered me about my new church home. All my friends could speak the same tongue as the youth pastor but I could not. On the contrary, I was speaking different kinds of tongues on different occasions. This became very uncomfortable for me because I wanted to be like all my friends. I wanted to speak the same or even similar tongues with the youth pastor. Moreover, I believed that because they were in a Pentecostal church for much longer than I, they must know more truths about this subject of speaking in tongues.

My language in tongues grew very much such that I even started singing in other tongues. I didn't know what was happening with me and sometimes it was scary for me. I could dance while praising God in tongues and some people in the church looked at me in a strange manner every time after worship. I felt uncomfortable, but didn't know what to do because I could not control what different kinds of tongues I would speak and how it would affect my body reaction. I could speak tongues as if I am battling something. I could be wrought with weariness or I could speak in a language so clearly that I could remember some words I used. Every time there was a conference, I would experience a deeper level of prayer in my tongue language. My vocabulary would increase; I even could understand some of the words I was saying. This was very exciting but scary at the same time because I knew especially from my non-Pentecostal background that praying in tongues was an extremely controversial subject.

This led me to the scriptures to find answers as to why do I seem to speak different tongues on different occasions. This took me time in asking, seeking and studying the Word of truth. Then to my surprise, I discovered two different and seemly opposing viewpoints. I found both these viewpoints in the book of first Corinthians.

The first viewpoint is found in **(1 Corinthians 14: 2 NIV):**

> *"For any one who speaks in a tongue does not speak to men but to God, indeed, no one understands him, he utters mysteries with his Spirit."*

In the first viewpoint, the scripture shows us that the mysteries uttered when speaking in tongues are not for anyone to understand for the Spirit speaks mysteries to God the Father.

Then another scripture in the same book of first Corinthians brings in another viewpoint as shown below:

> *"For if I pray in a tongue, my spirit prays, but my understanding is unfruitful."*
> **(1 Corinthians 14:14 NKJV).**

This showed me another truth to mean that my mind also cannot not understand the mysteries my spirit communicates with the Father.

This truth was so liberating yet confusing. It was confusing because it brought in questions like: *"How then can I know what I am praying for? What are these mysteries my spirit communicates with the Father?"* The two scriptures above gave me some form of a relief in my understanding. They revealed to me that my mind does not always have to know what my spirit is communicating with God. However, the same two scriptures still left me with unanswered questions. Further down the same passage of scripture in verse 27, the scripture seems to contradict itself from the first two verses above. The two scriptures above declare that neither my friend nor I understand. Nevertheless, verse 27 declares as shown below that someone must interpret the tongues. See below:

> **"If anyone speaks in a tongue, let them be two or at the most three, each in turn and let one interpret."**
> **(1 Corinthians 14:27 NKJV).**

This made me ask, *"But how can we interpret words we do not understand?"* The two scripture above put it clearly that the mind is unfruitful and understands nothing. There must be a mystery about this, the first verse says that when I am speaking in a tongue I am not speaking to men but my spirit communicates with God. Even my mind is not fruitful to understand these spiritual things. *"How then can I interpret things I don't understand?"* In trying to solve this mystery, the Lord took me to the scriptures in the same book of 1st Corinthians. The Lord gave me revelation to understand the scripture below as the answer to my questions. Look

76

carefully at these two verses. I meditated analytically upon them and challenge you to do the same.

> *"To another miraculous powers, to another prophesy, to another distinguishing between spirits, to another speaking in different KINDS of TONGUES and still another the interpretation of TONGUES."*
>
> **(1 Corinthians 12:10 NIV).**

> *And God has appointed these in the church: first apostles, second prophets, third teachers, after that miracles, then gifts of healings, helps, administrations, VARIETIES OF TONGUES."*
>
> **(1 Corinthians 12:28 NKJV).**

These two scriptures from the different versions of the Bible gave me more understanding in respect to the subject of tongues. The NIV used the words *"different kinds of tongues"* and the NKJV used the word *"varieties of tongues,"* the KJV used the word *"diversities of tongues."* In addition, the Amplified version used the word *"various kinds of (unknown) tongues."* This was evidence enough for me to see that there are different kinds of tongues.

If you first follow analytically the words used, you will also see that there are **DIFFERENT KINDS OF TONGUES**. The Lord then revealed to me that they are different kinds of tongues, which operate by different rules. With different uses, there are tongues I can interpret and tongues I cannot interpret. Hence, if there are different kinds of tongues then let us study more about them.

Tongues of Praising and Magnifying God

I remember the days just after being baptised in the Holy Spirit. I had just started speaking in other tongues. The experience was very exciting; I just wanted to speak in tongues all the time. The more I spoke in other tongues, the more I experienced different kinds of tongues and noticed that my vocabulary increased. All this simply encouraged me to speak in tongues all the more.

There were times when I was at church during praise and worship, that I would be lost in the presence of God. I would sing and worship in other tongues as I danced along the side of the sanctuary. These were some of my best moments in praise and worship. I enjoyed every moment of the service because the Spirit would fill me with joy and expectation throughout the service after such praise and worship. At times, I would even feel embarrassed because I was slain in the Holy Ghost repeatedly whenever there was good praise and worship. I did not know that the power that lied in magnifying God in the Spirit was the source of the miraculous.

Many worship leaders flow in the tongues of praising and magnifying; they will sing in the Spirit and also sing in understanding. The tongues of praise lead many people who flow in them into dancing in the Spirit, worshiping and ministering to God at levels higher than the natural. It would lead them into doing what they would ordinarily never do under normal circumstances. The account of Paul and Silas when in prison gives us more insight into the power of praising in the Spirit. The earthquake that destroyed the jail where the two were held was caused by the power of praising and magnifying in the Spirit. **(Acts 16:25-26)**. The apostle Paul even thanked God that he spoke in tongues more than everyone else. **(1 Corinthians 14:15).**

The book of Acts gives us more insight into what magnifying God entails:

> *"For they heard them speak with tongues, and MAGNIFY God ··· "*
>
> *(Act 10:46 NKJV).*

The word **"magnify"** as used in the King James Version of the Bible comes from a Greek word **"MEGALUNO"** which means; to *make great, to declare great, to increase and to extol*. Magnifying God can be done in other tongues and also in words we understand. In tongues, we can declare the greatness of God more accurately because we do it in the Spirit. The Spirit searches the deep things of God that natural words cannot express. Praying in the Spirit, therefore, gives us the ability to enjoy deep communion with the Father. We should pray in the Spirit and also in understanding. In understanding, we should always pray under the influence of the Spirit. We must always pray in the Spirit first so that our prayer in understanding comes under the influence of the Spirit.

I like the way Apostle Paul concluded this matter in **(1 Corinthians 14: 15 NKJV):**

> *"What is the conclusion then? I will pray with the Spirit, and I will also pray with understanding. I will sing with the Spirit, and I will also sing with understanding. "*

This conclusion gives us the entire picture of what praise and worship should look like. It should always be in Spirit and in truth. In Spirit is always praying in other tongues and in truth is praying in understanding but in-line with the Word of God, which is truth.

Man's relationship with God is limited to the revelation man has about God. We mostly relate to God based on His attributes. *"We know God you are good! God you're awesome!"* Yet we do not know the extent of His goodness. We cannot fathom His awesomeness. This is not personal. It is not born from intimacy. We tend to relate to God mostly through the senses, (i.e. things we can hear, things we can see, thing we can touch, things we can feel, and things we can smell). These things are very limited in showing us who God is. Since God is Spirit, we cannot possibly understand God with our natural senses. We need the Spirit who searches the deep things of God, to help us relate with God in ways deep and intimate. Our worship and praise must be born from the Spirit, because the Spirit knows the deep things of God so He can lead us in all truth in our worship. He can open up our spiritual senses and revolutionize our spiritual walk.

> **But God hath revealed them unto us by his Spirit: for the Spirit searcheth all things, yea, the deep things of God.**
> **(1Corinthians 2:10).**

When we magnify God in the Spirit, our fleshly motives and cravings are not involved because the mind is unfruitful. For my mind does not understand what my spirit through the Holy Spirit says to the Lord. ***"I say then: Walk in the Spirit, and you shall not fulfil the lust of the flesh."*** *(Galatians 5:16 NKJV).* This is the very reason why when we worship in the Spirit, we worship in the will of God. For the Spirit leads us in all truth. ***"Howbeit when he, the Spirit of truth, is come, he will guide you into all truth:..."*** *(John 16:13).* The Spirit of truth will guide our spirits and minds into all truth. He, the Spirit of truth, will align our minds and spirit with the will of God. This is the reason we need to pray in the Spirit before we pray in understanding. When we pray in tongues, the Holy Spirit reveals deep truths of God in our minds and spirits and causes us to pray in understanding in the will of God.

The Spirit gives us the ability to magnify God to the levels to which He is meant to be magnified. This is because the Spirit of truth knows and understands the Father as they are one.

Tongues of Prophesy

"And when Paul had laid hands on them, the Holy Spirit came upon them; and they spoke with tongues and PROPHESIED."
(Acts 19: 6 NKJV).

The word used for Prophesied in the above scripture comes from a Greek word **"PROPHETEUO."** This word propheteuo means *"to foretell events."* The scripture above therefore means that when they spoke in other tongues, they foretold the coming events in a spiritual language. This word from the Lord was then prophesied in understanding or interpretation so that all would know that which was spoken. The Lord gives a word to the body of Christ in a spiritual tongue for the purposes of correction, edification, teaching, or exhortation. This type of tongue must always be interpreted, because it is for the edification of all.

> *"How is it then, brethren? Whenever you come together, each has a psalm, has a teaching, has a TONGUE, has a revelation, has an interpretation. Let all things be done for edification."*
> **(1 Corinthians 14: 26 NKJV).**

Words given in the public arena MUST be interpreted or they are devoid of purpose. God always has purpose in what He does. He will not prompt you by His Spirit to give a word if He does not intend to provide its meaning. This is accomplished either immediately by the initial speaker of the word or it can be interpreted by another member of the body. This is because the church will not get anything from your message until there is an interpretation in a familiar language. For this reason, the gift of prophetic tongues always comes with the gift of interpretation.

A typical example from the scripture of how personal interpretation works is in the book of Ezekiel.

> *"The hand of the LORD was on me, brought me by the Spirit of the LORD, and made me rest in the midst of a valley, and it was full of bones."*
>
> *"Again He said to me, prophesy to these bones, and say to them, O dry bones, hear the word of the LORD."*

Different "Kinds" of Tongues

> *"So I prophesied as I was commanded, as I prophesied, there was a noise. And BEHOLD, there was a shaking! And the bones came near, a bone to it's bone."*

> *"And He said to me, prophesy to the Spirit, prophesy, son of man, and say the Spirit, so says the Lord Jehovah: come from the four winds, O Spirit, and breath on those dead ones so that they may live."*

> *"So I prophesied as He commanded me, and the Spirit came into them, and they lived and stood on their feet, an exceeding great army."*
>
> **(Ezekiel 37:1, 4, 7, 9 and 10 NKJV).**

The above scriptures show us that the Spirit first told the prophet what to say to the bones and the spirits. The prophet just followed the words of prophesy that were prophesied by the Spirit. The Spirit of the Lord prophesied and gave him utterance. All the prophet did was to say what the Spirit commanded in his language. This is how tongues of prophesy operate. The Spirit speaks in His language concerning things present or things to come, then He gives understanding and utterance to an individual to speak the words to the church in a language the church understands.

There are seasons when I frequently function in these kinds of prophesies. In these instances, I will speak a message in other tongues to the church. Immediately following, I will know what the Spirit said through my spirit and relay this understanding. An example of when another person interprets the word was a time during one of our Christ Ambassadors outreach team's meetings, the Lord prompted Brother Elisha to speak to us in tongues and then brother Shadreck immediately gave the interpretation to the tongues spoken by Brother Elisha. This is the true meaning of church responding to the voice of the same Holy Spirit. Many scriptures show passages where brethren are encouraged to give hymns, and songs, tongues and then others interpret the tongues as seen below.

> *"But now, brethren, if I come to you speaking with tongues, what shall I profit you unless I speak to you either by revelation, by knowledge, by prophesying, or by teaching."*
>
> **(1 Corinthians 14: 6 NKJV).**

Tongues are only understood either by interpretation or by revelation for they are a spiritual language. In this kind of ministry of tongues of prophesy, interpretation and revelation of tongues is a must because the core of this ministry is edification. Interpretation happens when one literally interprets the word spoken in a tongue into a language known by the listeners. On the other hand, revelation happens when one reveals the insight of the tongue; reveals the meaning or heart of the sayings. Most of the time, interpretation and revelation of tongues demands action to be taken concerning particular issues.

You cannot speak in a tongue TO THE CHURCH unless you can interpret or there is someone to interpret, and there is NO exception to this. However, this does not mean that you cannot pray to God in tongues in a church assembly. Whenever you gather in His Name to fellowship, pray more in tongues to God. Nevertheless, when the Lord gives you a word in tongues for the whole body you MUST always interpret this word into a language the body understands. This is to fulfil the condition of edification to the church.

> *"If anyone speaks in a tongue, let there be two or at the most three, each in turn, and let one interpret ······."*
> **(1 Corinthians 14: 27 NKJV).**

> *"But if there is no interpreter, let him keep silent in church, and let him speak to himself and to God."*
> **(1 Corinthians 14: 28 NKJV).**

Tongues of Edification

> *"But you beloved, building yourself up in your most holy faith, praying in the Holy Spirit."*
> **(Jude 20 NKJV).**

The above passage of scripture is very interesting in the sense that it brings together two core elements of a believers' life: The Word of God and the Holy Spirit of God. These elements form the head and the heart of every believer. A believer cannot do without the Word of God for faith comes from the Word. A believer cannot equally live without the Holy Spirit for the Spirit is the one who gives life. The life of God in us is by the Spirit of God.

"Being born again, not of corruptible seed, but of incorruptible, by the word of God, which liveth and abideth forever."

(1 peter 1:23).

Every believer is born of the Word and by the Spirit of God. This means that the Word and the Spirit of God together sustains every believer. The Lord Jesus brought it out so clearly in the book of **John 3:6** when He said:

"That which is born of the flesh is flesh; and that which is born of the Spirit is spirit."

(John 3:6).

The Word therefore is the building blocks that mix with the Holy Spirit as you pray in the Spirit (tongues) to build your spirit up into the image of God, in the most holy faith. Every believer born of the Word and the Spirit must therefore feed regularly on the Word of God and pray more often in the Spirit to grow spiritually. The Lord Jesus in *Matthew 4* said in response to the devil, *"That man shall not live on bread alone but on every Word that proceeds from the mouth of God."*

The fact that we are born of the Word and the Spirit, we need to feed on the Word and pray in the Spirit to be sustainable in our new nature. This kind of praying in the Spirit is a type of tongue that is given to everyone that believes. This is a personal tongue available to the whole body of Christ primarily for the purposes of self-edification. When Jesus said, *"they shall speak in other tongues"* as a sign of being believers in the book of **Mark 16:17**, He was referring to these tongues. This tongue of self-edification provides everyone with equal chances for growth in the kingdom. *"I returned, and* *saw under the sun, that the race is not to the swift, nor the battle to the strong, neither yet bread to the wise, nor yet riches to men of understanding, nor yet favour to men of skill; but time and chance happeneth to them all. "* *(Ecclesiastes 9:11).*

> **"He who speaks in a tongue EDIFIES himself…"**
> **(1 Corinthians 14:4 NKJV).**

The word **edify** comes from a Greek word which means **to construct, to build, to embolden.** Speaking in other tongues builds you up into the image of God. Your life opens up more to spiritual activities. You invite heaven to do business with you. Speaking in tongues opens you to angelic activities in your life; as you speak in tongues, you invite angels to fight your battles and open more doors to spiritual realms. Tongues gives you mastery over the enemy and all his vices because you have adopted the heavenly language. It enables you to function from the heavenly platform, thereby superceding the enemy's plans and schemes.

You build yourself into a Spiritual giant the more you speak in other tongues. Speaking in other tongues gives you the ability to function in the spiritual reality; it makes you operate in all the nine (9) gifts of the Spirit and makes you function in all the sevenfold manifestation of the Holy Spirit. People who walked closer to the Lord spoke more in other tongues than usual. These people built themselves up into giants in the Spirit through speaking in tongues. Paul, the great apostle, said that he prayed more in tongues than anyone else. Catherine Khulman said she prayed more in other tongues. Benny Hinn says he prays more in tongues.

Kenneth E. Hagin said he prayed more in tongues. Pastor Chris Oyakhilome prays in more tongues. Name a spiritual giant in this age or the ages that past, I will most likely show you a frequent tongue talker.

Tongues of Intercession

"Praying always with all prayer and supplication in the Spirit, being watchful to this end with all perseverance and supplication FOR all saints."
(Ephesians 6:18 NKJV).

There are two different manifestations of this kind of tongues. One type manifests in a normal Spiritual language like all other tongues. The other type comes in groans that words cannot express. The type mentioned in the opening scripture above, is a type of intercession in the Spirit, which is just a normal tongue of spiritual words.

Interceding in tongues avails us with an opportunity to progress the will of the Lord in places and situations which necessitate it. The Lord may need prayer invested in a particular place and situation so that He can deliver or save. Then, He, the Lord of grace, will give a burden on someone to pray. This usually happens with those who yield themselves to the Spirit and prayer. You can be praying here in South Africa and save a life in India. Your prayers in tongues go a long way in fulfilling God's will in many people's lives across the world. The eyes of the Lord run to and fro looking for people who pray in the Spirit, people He can place a burden on to pray and defuse situations around the cities and Nations of the world. Oftentimes people drop themselves into many different problems and circumstances because of lack of wisdom and knowledge. The Lord, because of His mercy, always looks for people to pray so that He can deliver them.

Back home in Zambia, after the very controversial presidential elections, there was a thick tension fuming in the air. The very same night, the Lord gave me a dream depicting utter chaos in the city. There were angry riots that lead to bloodshed taking place as violence took over. My dream was so vivid that I even saw a specific young man killed in the stampede. This was such a horrible site that I was very disturbed by it the whole night and day. When returning from work the following day, I saw the very same young man I had dreamed of the previous night. My heart and spirit grieved, I called to him and gave him some money, which I had prayed over, so that the money could act as a contact point. Upon reaching the Christ Ambassadors meeting, I shared the dream with the team and we prayed in other tongues and broke and defused the whole incidence in the Spirit.

The scripture declares that we wrestle not against flesh and blood but against principalities in the heavenly places. Before anything happens in the physical, there is an occurrence in the spiritual realm in the heavenly places. Those who are spiritually sensitive will know what is to happen and can defuse the situation in the spirit before it manifests in the physical realm. The police were able to defuse the incidence the following day even before it gained momentum. Glory be to God that He used our prayers of intercession to diffuse the incidence and cancel the plans of the enemy. Praying in tongues is indeed a powerful tool!

Groaning in the Spirit

The second type of tongues of intercession comes in form of groans that cannot be expressed in words. This kind of tongues only comes when there is a serious situation about to happen. These tongues come to people as a burden for family or friends who are facing a life or death situation. This can be physical or spiritual death. These tongues carry the resurrection power of God. These tongues can be given to you by the Spirit to pray for someone who is about to die physically or spiritually or they can be for a person who's facing some adverse circumstances and needs the Lord to preserve their lives.

> *"Likewise the Spirit also helps in our weaknesses. For we do not know what we should pray as we ought, but the Spirit Himself makes intercession for us with groanings which cannot be uttered."*
> **(Romans 8:26 NKJV).**

There are many times we do not know what to pray for because of our many limitations. For instance, we are not omnipresent to know what is happening everywhere. We are not physically capable of being everywhere at once. We are also not all knowing so we need the Spirit, who knows everything, to help us with what to pray for and for whom to pray. The Spirit of God is omnipresent and all knowing because God the Father is and they are one. The Holy Spirit sometimes will not tell us for whom or what specifically we are to pray. In these instances,

He will instill an unshakable burden to pray which manifests as groanings not expressible in words.

Groanings come from a place of identification; a place of being in the very place and situation of the person for whom you are praying. The Spirit takes you into a place of identification and makes you hate the infirmity with a passion. The Lord Jesus identified with the pain of losing a brother when the sisters of Lazarus came to Him mourning their brother's death.

> *"Therefore, when Jesus saw her weeping and the Jews who came with her weeping, He GROANED in the Spirit and was troubled."*
> **(John 11:33 NKJV).**

> *"Then Jesus, again GROANING in Himself, came to the tomb. It was a cave, and a stone lay against it."*
> **(John 11:38 NKJV).**

Like the Lord Jesus, these kinds of tongues of groaning come from a place of compassion. Identification always leads to compassion. Compassion leads to desperation and a holy anger against the infirmity. Groanings in the Spirit are born from a place of compassion. The Lord Jesus had compassion on the death of Lazarus and groaned in the Spirit to resurrect him. I remember one time a young man came to a Christ Ambassadors meeting. This young man of about 19years of age came to me with a back problem, which he had for over five years. He explained that he had gone to the hospital several times over the years and recently resorted to witchdoctors because he got no help from the hospital.

When he came for the meeting one Thursday evening and explained the whole problem to me, I was overwhelmed with compassion. At that point, the young man could not even sit on a desk at school. He had to lean on something every time. I felt so moved in my spirit that I went to pray for him later in the night. However, something strange happened to me when I was praying for him. The moment I started praying, I all of the sudden had this terrible back pain. Then immediately I started to groan in the Spirit. I felt like someone with very real back problems. I was in searing pain and groaned for about an hour. Then I got the breakthrough, I felt liberated, loosed and the back pains disappeared.

The following day during the meeting, I called him for prayer and I was relaxed because I knew I already won the battle in the spirit. When I prayed for him, he screamed, fell and laid on the floor for about five minutes. He then woke up and gave us a testimony that he saw three men working on his back when he was lying on the floor. At one point he said, *"I wanted to get up but the men told me that they had not yet finished working on me. Therefore, I lay back down until they finished working on me. After some time they all stood up and waved at me, then I woke up."* From that moment on, the boy was totally healed. He is now a high school graduate and is working for a construction company carrying heavy loads with his once fragile back. God totally healed and restored the young man, to the Praise of His Glory!

Another incidence happened when I was staying in Chudliegh, one of Lusaka city suburbs. One day after work, I came home and was watching some sermons on DVD. After a while I started praying, just praising and worshiping God. Then suddenly, I had a very heavy burden on me and immediately started groaning in the Spirit. I groaned for about two and a half hours and then I got relief. Five minutes later, I received a phone call from my brother telling me that robbers had attacked my parents' home. They had actually entered one of the quarters and held the people in that quarter hostage. The Lord gave me a burden to pray for my family and probably to protect their lives. If I had ignored the burden and did not pray, my brother in law could have died as he was hit from behind in the neck with a machete. By God's grace, the machete did not touch the spinal cord and the robbers ran away without getting anything from the house.

Groaning in the Spirit with words that cannot be uttered spared my family's lives. Glory to God!

> *"Cretans and Arabs ---- we hear them speaking in our own tongues the wonderful works of God."*
>
> **(Acts 2:11 NKJV).**

This kind of tongues comes in the form of a language that belongs to a specific people group. This mainly happens when God wants to communicate certain truths to His people using a person who has influence and understanding but does not know the vernacular of that particular people. In such instances, the person speaking a foreign language receives divine understanding of the language he is speaking. However, there are some instances when the person used to speak in a foreign language does not understand the language.

I have had many instances, when praying in other tongues, in which the language was so clear to me that I knew the meanings of the words used. Several times, I would later discover, I found that the words I used were from a particular language. One of the words I can recall is "**YADA**" which is a Hebrew word meaning, "**to know in an intimate way**". I have also worshiped in a language I believe to be Hebrew, especially when singing in other tongues.

> *"And when this sound occurred, the multitudes came together, and were confused, because everyone heard them speak his own language. Then they were all amazed and marveled, saying to one another, "look, are not all these who speak Galileans? "And how is it that we hear, each in our own language in which we were born?"*
>
> **(Acts 2:6, 7, 8 NKJV).**

Here in the scripture above we see that the people from all over were surprised at how the Galileans would speak their mother tongues or languages fluently.

One of the testimonies I heard about this kind of tongues is from one prophet by the name of Perry Stone. I heard him speaking on TV once explaining how his father could preach in a language he could not naturally know. A language he did not even understand. God could give him utterance to preach in a language he did not know. He could get to a place to preach and not need an interpreter because the Spirit gave him utterance to speak many languages with supernatural fluency. Another example is of my young brother Shadreck, so

94

gifted and anointed in many ways. He was speaking in tongues as he was praying one day at church. When the service was over, a certain woman walked to him and asked him when and how he had learned to speak French so fluently? My brother cannot speak French at all under normal earthly circumstances, but in the Spirit, all languages are accessible.

Apostle Paul declared, "That all things are yours," (1 Corinthians 3:21) and if he was talking to a new creation like I am, then I also declare by the power of the Holy Ghost that all things are mine in Christ Jesus! This includes all languages of this world. God is the one who gave and separated the languages. These languages are occasionally availed to us by the Holy Ghost for the advancement of the Kingdom of God. Hallelujah!

Part 2

Understanding the Power of Tongues

He that speaketh in an unknown tongue edifieth himself.

8

Sovereignty of Speaking In Tongues

𝒯ongues are not an earthly language; therefore, they do not operate in a time zone. Tongues do not function in tenses such as past tense, present tense, or future tense. This is because tongues operate in eternity. They are heavenly languages that function outside the operation of time. This means that in tongues, one can speak and affect things in the past, present and future. In tongues, you have power to change the past, present and the future events. Tongues operate in the realm of God. God knows the beginning from the end of everything. He is not limited by time. God is not limited by past, present or future, because He operates from eternity, which is outside the operation of time. He's got time in His hands and therefore cannot be controlled by time. He is God over time as well. He can choose to operate in or outside of time at will. The Lord Jesus declares in the scripture in the book of revelations that He is the beginning and the end. This means that everything starts and ends with Him. The same way he who operates in the realm of tongues operates in the realm of eternity. One would wonder why it is necessary to change events in the past. The past holds the key to the future. Therefore, it is very important to change the past in order to reap a good future. The Bible is full of genealogies to show just how much important the past is to the future. Man always reaps what he sows. Man always inherits from his father's blessings or curses. Jesus appeared in the genealogy of men to redeem man from the curses of the past that flowed through man's blood (Mathew 1:1-16). He joined the genealogy of men with a different kind of blood to change the past and the future of men. When you become born again your past is not only changed but it is erased. This is the main reason why Jesus Christ the son of God came into this world to create us a new, without a past but with a present and a future. *"Therefore if any man be in Christ, he is a new creature: old things are passed away; behold, all things are become new."* (2 Corinthians 5:17).

Many people today have inherited blessings and curses alike from the past. Many have inherited royalty, wealth and more from the hard work or sacrifices of generations that passed on. The Lord's blessing follows in the generations that succeed. Similarly, curses follow the generations that succeed. Many suffer from the consequences of their past. Many suffer from curses provoked in the past. The rituals participated in and the generational problems brought down from the past affect them now. If you identify yourself with having difficulties rooted in any of the problems from your past, I have good news for you. In tongues, under the power of the Holy Spirit, it is possible to uproot things in your past and plant good seeds of good words in order to reap a good future.

> *"Then the Lord put forth his hand, and touched my mouth. And the Lord said unto me, Behold, I have put my <u>words</u> in thy mouth. See, I have this day set thee over the nations and over the kingdoms, to root out, and to destroy, and to throw down, to build, and to plant."*
> **(Jeremiah 1:9-10 NJKV).**

The scripture above declares that with the words received from the Spirit of the Lord, we have power over the nations and the kingdoms of the world. In tongues, we use divine words and language from the Lord, which is higher than the languages of this world. These words have power to uproot wrong seeds planted in our lives. Power to destroy every wrong foundation our lives are built upon. Power to build ourselves up into spiritual giants and to plant seeds of divine words. These, in turn, are able to build us up into the wisdom of the heavenlies and create for ourselves a desired future.

All you have to do is put your mind on the situation you want to change and the seed or curse you want to destroy. Then pray in tongues about it and start uprooting and destroying everything in your life through your confessions. If you put your mind on events that happened in the past and pray in tongues about it, you will be able to uproot the cause of the problem and not just the effects. All prayer in tongues must be in the Name of Jesus. Many people today are struggling because of words spoken to them in the past. Many struggle with things done to them in the past. I have good news for you. If you are struggling with your past, in tongues you will not only do away with the pain but also uproot the cause. This has the ability to change your whole being; spirit, soul and body. This will bring you total healing and give you new and better prospects for the future.

Unsearchable Things Unveiled When Speaking in Tongues

In tongues, great and hidden things promised by the Lord the Father of our Lord Jesus Christ are unveiled. The Lord of Heavens invited us who seek Him, to call on Him and He will answer and show us things unsearchable with our ordinary minds. The righteous father gave this invitation through prophet Jeremiah as shown below:

> *"Call to me and I will answer you and tell you great and unsearchable things you do not know."*
>
> **(Jeremiah 33:3 NIV).**

The Lord answered and granted this promise to those who seek Him through the tool of speaking in tongues. The scripture declares that he who speaks in tongues speaks mysteries. These mysteries are the *"unsearchable things"* the scripture above refers to. In tongues, we speak deep and unsearchable things in the Holy Spirit.

Through the interpretation and the revelation of tongues, we get to understand the mysteries, the deep things of God. The scriptures below show us that only the Spirit of God can reveal these deep things to us.

Therefore, we can only understand these deep things with the aid of the Holy Spirit through the tool of speaking in tongues.

> *"But as it is written, Eye hath not seen, nor ear heard, neither have entered into the heart of man, the things which God hath prepared for them that love him. <u>But God hath revealed them unto us by his Spirit</u>: for the Spirit searcheth all things, yea, the deep things of God. For what man knoweth the things of a man, save the spirit of man which is in him? even so the things of God knoweth no man, but the Spirit of God. Now we have received, not the spirit of the world, but the spirit which is of God; that we might know the things that are freely given to us of God. Which things also we speak, not in the words which man's wisdom teacheth, but which the Holy Ghost teacheth; comparing spiritual things with spiritual."*
>
> **(1 Corinthians 2:9-13).**

Some interesting spiritual principles are unlocked in the scripture above. The deep and unsearchable things we do not know are the things that *"Eye hath not seen, nor ear heard, neither have entered into the heart of man, the things which God hath prepared for them that love him."* The first key to unlock these things is in the line which declares, *"The Spirit searches all things, even the deep things of God."* The deep and unsearchable things prophesied by the Lord through prophet Jeremiah are now accessible to those who love the Lord by the Holy Spirit. The Holy Spirit searches the deep things of God from within us.

The other key to this mystery is in the line which declares, *"We have not received the spirit of the world but the Spirit who is from God, that we may know what God has freely given us."* The Spirit who lives within us gives us the ability to know the deep and unsearchable things freely given to us.

The third key unlocked is that we know these deep and unsearchable things through speaking, as shown in the line which declares *"This is what we SPEAK, not in WORDS taught us by human wisdom but in WORDS taught by the Spirit, expressing spiritual truths in spiritual WORDS."* In tongues, we express spiritual truths in spiritual words. These truths are the deep and unsearchable things we do not know naturally.

One of the biggest mysteries unlocked is that we know the deep things of God through speaking. In tongues, the Spirit of God reveals the deep truths and revelations to our spirits. Through speaking in tongues the Holy Spirit reveals deep and unsearchable things into our spirits as shown in the line which declares *"However, as it is written: "No eye has seen, no ear has heard, no mind has conceived what God has prepared for those who love him" but God has revealed it to us by his Spirit."*

These truths are the unsearchable things we do not know naturally. These spiritual words are referred to as speaking in other tongues in the books of **Acts 2:4 and 1 Corinthians 13:1.**

Our Place of Refuelling-Tongues

Tongues provide a place of refuge, a resting place, a place of Spiritual refreshing. As we speak in other tongues, we enter a spiritual place of deep and holy rest. This replenishes our spirit, soul, and body and causes us to live lives free from the stress of this world. As we constantly live in this place of speaking in tongues, our youth is constantly renewed. We develop worry and stress resistant lives. We live lives of constant rest regardless of the situation or circumstances.

When we mix the discipline of studying the Word of God and speaking in tongues, we will develop a holy cushion that cushions our hearts and minds with the peace of God regardless of what happens.

> *"Very well, with foreign lips and strange tongues God will speak to this people, to whom He said, "This is the RESTING-PLACE, let WEARY REST"; and, This is the place of repose" ..."*
>
> **(Isaiah 28:11-12 NIV).**

Tongues provide a place where the weary, the burned out find rest. This rest comes from the communion between our spirits and the Holy Spirit as we speak in tongues. Speaking in tongues gets us refreshed from the inner man. This results from the communion between the inner man and the Holy Spirit.

> *"But he that is joined unto the Lord is one spirit."*
>
> **(1Corinthians 6:17).**

"For by one Spirit are we all baptized into one body, whether we be Jews or Gentiles, whether we be bond or free; and HAVE BEEN ALL MADE TO DRINK INTO ONE SPIRIT."
(1Corinthians 12:13).

Many people in the world use alcohol, drugs, sex, and many other vices to relieve themselves from stress. These vices only manage to renew the flesh and might be costly to our lives and families. Sometimes even good things like exercise will not fully free us from the troubles of our lives. *"For bodily exercise profiteth little: but godliness is profitable unto all things, having promise of the life that now is, and of that which is to come."* (*1 Timothy 4:8*).

Tongues will give us rest free from the cost to life and family. When you are weary and burned out, just spare time to pray in tongues. You will then see how mighty and powerful tongues can be for stress management

Holiness of Tongues

"But ye beloved, building up yourselves on your most HOLY faith, praying in the Holy Ghost."

(Jude 20).

Faith comes from hearing the Word of God. Faith is putting to work what we believe in the Word of God. Righteousness comes from believing the Word of God and faith comes from doing the Word of God. Faith is therefore in the realm of righteousness because it comes from the Word of God. Faith is simply the walk of righteousness.

> *"For with the heart man believeth unto righteousness..."*
>
> **(Romans 10:10).**

If faith comes from the realm of righteousness, how then does the Most Holy Faith come about? Taking into account that faith comes from righteousness, which originates from the ways of God and not holiness that originates from the works of God.

The Psalmist in Psalm 145:17 declared, *"The Lord is righteous in all his ways and holy in all his works."* The scripture above shows us that Holiness is in the works of God and Righteousness is in the ways of God.

This, therefore, means that holiness has nothing to do with ways but works of the Holy Spirit. Through praying in tongues, the ways and the works of God meet in one place to form the most holy faith. Faith comes from the Word at work in you and holiness comes from the Holy Spirit at work in you. The process of speaking in tongues makes the Word and the Holy Spirit to form a faith that has both the ways and the works of God in one. This is what we call the Most Holy Faith.

Holiness has everything to do with separation; anything declared holy is set apart or consecrated. Tongues are separated ways of praying to God, separate from the languages of this world. By praying in the Spirit you build your faith in a consecrated way, in a pure way, a separated way, a holy way. Praying in tongues builds your faith based on the purity of the Word and the works of God and not on experiences or testimonies of others. This kind of praying produces works, which are holy and set apart.

Language of Zion
(Heavenly Jerusalem)

"But ye are come unto mount Zion, and unto the City of the living God, the heavenly Jerusalem, and to an innumerable company of angels, To the general assembly and church of the firstborn, which is written in heaven, and to God the Judge of all, and to the spirits of just men made perfect, And to Jesus the mediator of the new covenant, and to the blood of sparkling, that speaketh better things than that of Abel."

(Hebrews 12:22-24).

The scripture above declares that we have come to a spiritual place, to the heavenly Jerusalem. This is the city of the living God where we are in the company of angels. In this city, we communicate spiritual truths in spiritual languages. These spiritual languages are also known as the language of angels. 1 Corinthians 13:1 declares that we can speak the tongues of men and tongues of angels.

As we speak in other tongues, we speak into eternity. We operate at a level that transcends the realms of the mind, the level that is heavenly and goes beyond the wisdom of the world. We interact with the heavens as we speak in tongues, charging angels to do business with us. In tongues, we challenge heaven to deal with us as we are. Tongues create for us a home in the heavenly places; we become much more acquainted to our heavenly place through speaking in tongues. Tongues establish us in a place of influence and authority in the heavenly places and manifests this authority in the earth.

> *"For anyone who speaks in a tongue does not speak to men but to God. Indeed, no one understands him; he utters mysteries with his spirit."*
>
> **(1 Corinthians 14:2 NIV).**

Tongues are a mysterious language given to a mysterious people. A heavenly people who discuss things mysterious to this world and to the wisdom of this world. In tongues, we discuss certain mysterious truths that are important to God and heaven. We access new revelations from the heavens through speaking in tongues. We preserve the earth with the wisdom hidden in speaking in tongues. We change the cause of events on earth and the calendar of events in the heavens as we speak in tongues.

Speak more in tongues and participate in the affairs of the heavens. He who speaks in tongues does not speak to men but to God the Father and God of our Lord Jesus Christ. Glory to the highest heavens!

9

Power of Tongues for Edification

"He that speaketh in an unknown tongue edifieth himself... "

(1 Corinthians 14:4).

Edification comes from a Greek word **"OIKODOMEO"** that means among others *building a concrete structure, and to embolden.* This then means through speaking in tongues we can construct from our spirit, soul, and body a supernatural structure. We open our bodies to supernatural health; our lives to more of the realities of the spiritual as we speak more in tongues.

Speaking in tongues has the power to take us to a large place in the spiritual realm. In this place, our eyes of understanding open more to the realities of the heavenlies where we are seated with Christ. We become aware of our inheritance and take our proper place of authority in Christ, when we come to this large place.

The large place is a place of honour; it is a place of blessings. The story of the man called Jabez gives us an example of a man who understood the benefits of operating from the large place, the place of authority and influence. Here is the summary of Jabez's story as recorded in 1st Chronicles 4:9-10.

> *And Jabez was more honourable than his brethren: and his mother called his name Jabez, saying, Because I bare him with sorrow. And Jabez called on the God of Israel, saying, Oh that thou wouldest bless me indeed, and enlarge my coast, and that thine hand might be with me, and that thou wouldest keep me from evil, that it may not grieve me! And God granted him that which he requested.*

From the story of Jabez we can tell that in the large place there is a heavy anointing. We can also tell that there is grace to protect us from evil and sin. The edification that we get in tongues brings us to the large place. Influence, a heavy anointing settles on our lives and grace to overcome sin and evil. Like Jabez, the Lord can grant us this large territory as we pray in tongues.

> *"He brought me forth also into a large place; he delivered me, because he delighted in me. The LORD rewarded me according to my righteousness; according to the cleanness of my hands hath he recompensed me. For I have kept the ways of the LORD, and have not wickedly departed from my God.*

For all his judgments were before me, and I did not put away his statutes from me. I was also upright before him, and I kept myself from mine iniquity. Therefore hath the LORD recompensed me according to my righteousness, according to the cleanness of my hands in his eyesight. With the merciful thou wilt shew thyself merciful; with an upright man thou wilt shew thyself upright; With the pure thou wilt shew thyself pure; and with the froward thou wilt shew thyself froward. For thou wilt save the afflicted people; but wilt bring down high looks. For thou wilt light my candle: the LORD my God will <u>enlighten my darkness</u>. For by thee I have <u>run through a troop;</u> and by my God have I <u>leaped over a wall.</u> As for God, his way is perfect: the word of the LORD is tried: he is a buckler to all those that trust in him. For who is God save the LORD? or who is a rock save our God? It is God that <u>girdeth me with strength</u>, and <u>maketh my way perfect.</u> He maketh my feet like <u>hinds' feet,</u> and setteth me upon my high places. He teacheth my <u>hands to war</u>, so that a <u>bow of steel is broken by mine arms</u>. Thou hast also given me the <u>shield of thy salvation</u>: and thy right hand hath holden me up, and thy <u>gentleness hath made me great.</u> {thy gentleness...: or, with thy meekness thou <u>hast multiplied me}</u> Thou hast <u>enlarged my steps under me</u> that <u>my feet did not slip. I</u> have pursued mine enemies, and <u>overtaken them</u>: neither did I turn again till they were consumed. I have wounded them that they were not able to rise: they are fallen under my feet.

For thou hast <u>girded me with strength unto the battle</u>: thou hast subdued under me those that rose up against me. Thou hast also given me the necks of mine enemies; that I might destroy them that hate me. They cried, but there was none to save them: even unto the LORD, but he answered them not. Then did I beat them small as the dust before the wind: I did cast them out as the dirt in the streets. "

(Psalms 18:19-42).

The above scripture gives us a clear picture of what it means to be in a large place. Speaking in tongues takes us to this large place, as we receive edification. The highlights of the above scripture give us about 14 places where the Lord builds us in this process of edification.

Let us explore the 14 highlighted places of the above scripture and study in detail what the Lord wants to accomplish in us through the process of speaking in tongues. In the above scripture, we see that as we speak more in tongues the Lord begins to **enlighten areas of darkness** in our lives. The Amplified Bible puts it more clearly like this, **"For you cause my lamp to be lighted and to shine; the Lord my God illuminates my darkness. "** The lamp is the Word of God in your life **(Psalms 119:105)**. As you speak more in tongues, the Word of God in you starts to shine and discern areas of darkness in your life. The Word will enlighten dark areas and bring life in every area of your life **(Hebrews 4:12)**.

Then He will give you the ability through tongues to **"run through a troop"** which is the wall that was shutting you in. You receive by the Spirit through tongues the ability to run through situations that in the past have held you prisoner. The Lord, by the Spirit through speaking in tongues, also gives the ability to *"leap over a wall."* This is the ability to jump over the walls of limitations. He shall also *"buckle you with strength"* in your character by the Word and *"make your ways perfect"* as you speak more in tongues. The Lord will give you *"hind's feet"* which means He will give you the ability to stand firm and make progress in dangerous heights of testing and trouble.

The Lord will, through the process of edification, *"teach your hands to war"* so that you can be able to *"break the bow of steel"* by your hands. This strength is for spiritual warfare to quench the arrows and attacks of the devil that you receive as you speak more in tongues. The right hand of the Lord *becomes the shield of your salvation* and the gentleness of the Lord *becomes your greatness*. As you speak more in tongues, the Lord *"enlarges our steps and makes them firm."* This enlarging of your steps is spiritual expedience. You begin to do things at a supernatural speed. Just like the Prophet Elijah outran horses in his days, so shall you begin to outrun your odds. Things you do will gain divine speed and expedience. This then will give you the ability to overtake.

The large place is a place of spiritual strength and of supernatural occurrences. It is a place of greatness, enlarged steps, supernatural stability, and speed.

Speak more in tongues and enter into in your large place. Live the supernatural life naturally. Glory to the highest!

The Seed of Power

"Behold, I give unto you power to tread on serpents and scorpions, and over all the power of the enemy: and nothing shall by any means hurt you. "

(Luke 10:19).

The scripture above declares that the Lord Jesus has given us power (exousia) to overcome the works of the enemy. This power is given to believers the moment they are born again. Hence, the reason why the Lord Jesus in **Mark 16:17** declared that believers shall be able to cast out devils, lay hands on the sick and see them recovered.

"He that believeth and is baptized shall be saved; but he that believeth not shall be damned. And these signs shall follow them that believe; In my name shall they cast out devils; they shall speak with new tongues; They shall take up serpents; and if they drink any deadly thing, it shall not hurt them; they shall lay hands on the sick, and they shall recover. "

(Mark 16:16-18).

This authority given to every believer as recorded in the above scripture comes in seed form. In this form, the authority can grow in power to have the maximum results. For this seed to grow and manifest in you, you need to do the godly exercise of praying in the Spirit and meditating on the Word of God. The word power in the above scripture comes from a root word **"EXOUSIA."** Exousia is a Greek word that means, among other words, "competency and mastery."

This means the Lord has given us competency and mastery in our spirit against the forces of darkness. However, we have to grow this seed of power through the process of speaking in tongues and meditation on the Word of God in order to competently defeat the demonic powers of the enemy.

The other word used for power is the Greek word **"DUNAMIS,"** which means miraculous power. This is the power to do God's work. This power also comes in seed form. This is the mystery behind the miraculous, the seed aspect of the power given by the Holy Spirit.

> *"But ye shall receive POWER (DUNAMIS), after that the Holy Ghost is come upon you... "*
> **(Acts 1:8).**

> *"And behold, I send the promise of my father upon you: but tarry ye in the city of Jerusalem, until ye be endued with POWER (DUNAMIS) from on high."*
> **(Luke 24:49).**

Many believers in the body of Christ have received the Holy Spirit in their lives yet only few function in the miraculous power. This is because not many have the understanding that speaking in tongues or praying in the Spirit provides. It demonstrably grows the seed of the miraculous and gives the ability to do the wonderful works of God. The dunamis power gives you the ability to be a witness for Christ. It gives you the ability to perform miracles, signs and wonders. This ability, however, comes in seed form and can only be increased through the processes of meditation on the Word and speaking in tongues.

Speaking in tongues is a tool that unlocks the miraculous as well as gives you mastery over the forces of darkness and the wisdom of this world.

Roots Us in Love

The scriptures declare that the Holy Spirit poured the love of God into our hearts. The more we speak in tongues, the greater this love will grow into maturity.

> *"...because the love of God is shed abroad in our hearts by the Holy Ghost which is given to us."*
>
> **(Romans 5:5).**

The love shed in our hearts is a seed of love. This seed needs to be matured in order to grow in our lives. The full manifestation of this love shed in our hearts is the manifestation of Christ in our lives. This is because Christ is the manifested love of God.

> *"But after that the kindness and the <u>Love of God</u> our saviour toward man appeared."*
>
> **(Titus 3:4).**

Tongues are a mysterious tool the Holy Spirit uses to strengthen our inner man and shape our nature to be more like His. Every gift given by the Holy Spirit can only come into full maturity through the Holy Spirit's help. Speaking in tongues automatically taps you into the living pulse of the Spirit.

"For this cause I bow my knees unto the father of our Lord Jesus Christ, Of whom the whole family in heaven and earth is named, That he would grant you according to the riches of his glory, to be strengthened with MIGHT (Dunamis) by his Spirit in the inner man, That Christ may dwell in your hearts by faith; that ye , being rooted and grounded in love may be able to comprehend with all saints what is the breadth, and the length, and depth, and height, And to KNOW (gnosko) the love of Christ, which passeth KNOWLEDGE (gnosis), that ye might be filled all the fullness of God. "

(Ephesians 3:14-19).

The word **"know"** in the above passage of scripture comes from a Greek word **"GINOSKO"** which means having absolute knowledge, having a good perception; a good understanding in the Spirit of the love of Christ. On the contrary, the word **"knowledge"** in the scripture above comes from a root word **"GNOSIS"** which means scientific knowledge. This is the knowledge based on the scientific evidence of the understanding of the love of Christ. This knowledge is a lower kind of knowledge based on mental or physical understanding. God is Spirit and a natural mind cannot comprehend the full dynamics of His love. A natural man cannot have deep understanding of the love of God. Unless man has absolute knowledge, or divine revelation, which is only given by the Holy Spirit, he cannot comprehend the vastness of the love of God.

The strengthening of the inner man by the Holy Spirit through the exercise of speaking in tongues produces the ability to grow the love of Christ in you. As you speak more in tongues, you are rooted and grounded deeper in love. You understand the breadth, the length, the depth and the height of the love of God culminated in your heart. Then you will know the fullness of God in your spirit. Strengthen your inner man through constantly praying in tongues!

Builds Your Faith into the Most Holy Faith

"But ye, beloved, building up yourselves on your most holy faith, Praying in the Holy Ghost."

(Jude 20).

The words **"building up"** come from a Greek word **"EPOIKODOMEO,"** which means to build upon. This then means that as you pray in tongues, you begin to build upon your faith, the most holy faith. This is the highest level of faith in which one can operate. Build your faith upon the rock, which is the purity of the holiness of the truth in the Word of God.

Praying in tongues consecrates our faith into a supernatural structure. Our faith is built on the purity of the Word and the holiness of the Holy Spirit. We build our faith upon the testimonies of the Lord and lean upon His understanding.

┌─────────┐
│   │
│   10   │
│   │
└─────────┘

Power of Tongues for Praising and Magnifying

"Sacrifice has always been an imperative, yet sensitive subject to God from the time of Adam. God is very particular with the subject of sacrifice. We can see this in the way He accepted Able's sacrifice and rejected Cain's sacrifice. *"And Abel, he also brought of the firstlings of his flock and of the fat thereof. And the LORD had respect unto Abel and to his offering: But unto Cain and to his offering he had not respect. And Cain was very wroth, and his countenance fell."* **(Genesis 4:4-5).**

God preferred Able's sacrifice and rejected Cain's. He is very particular about the quality of sacrifice that is acceptable along with the consecrated attitude of the heart. The Lord God was also very specific with the animals used for sacrificial offering. He required sacrificial animals to be of a particular age, of a particular gender, and to be without spot or blemish. In other words, the sacrificial animal was supposed to be holy at all times. Sacrifice was always to be holy in God's eyes to be acceptable.

This is because God always had a picture of the perfect sacrifice in mind. Everything else would be just a shadow of the sacrifice He envisioned and therefore, would be insufficient for forgiveness. God required every animal sacrifice made through the shedding of its blood to represent the perfect sacrifice. The perfect sacrifice was holy, without spot and blemish so that He could satisfy the full requirements for sin. Jesus Christ was and is the perfect sacrifice. The giving of the perfect sacrifice in Jesus Christ made the sacrifice of animals to no longer be necessary. No animal could take the place that the Son of God did when He was sacrificed for us. Hence, the Psalmist prophesied in **Psalms 69:30-31:**

"I will praise the name of God with a song, and will magnify him with thanksgiving. This <u>ALSO SHALL</u> please the LORD better than an ox or bullock that hath horns and hoofs."

The psalmist used the word **"SHALL"** to show that this kind of sacrifice would happen in the future with the death and the resurrection of our Lord Jesus. With the death and resurrection of Christ Jesus who was the ultimate sacrifice, there is sacrifice from our lips and lifted hands (Psalms 141:2). Other passages of scripture like **Hosea 14:2** declares:

"Take with you words, and turn to the LORD: say unto him, Take away all iniquity, and receive us graciously: so will we render the calves of our lips."

Instead of animal sacrifice, the prophet admonished us to take with us words wrought from the soul, and turn to the Lord. The words we take to the Lord are also called the calves of our lips. **Hebrews 13:15** also ascribes to the sacrifice of our lips as shown below:

> *"By him therefore let us offer the sacrifice of praise to God continually, that is, the fruit of our lips giving thanks to his name."*
> **(Hebrews 13:15).**

Sacrifice offered to God must be without spot and blemish to be acceptable. The old covenant animal sacrifice was a shadow of the new covenant fruit offering of our lips. If the shadow was blameless, then the real sacrifice must be blameless as well. During the old covenant, sacrifice could be rejected by God. In the new covenant, sacrifice can likewise be rejected.

> *"I beseech you therefore, brethren, by the mercies of God, that ye present your bodies a living sacrifice, holy, <u>acceptable unto God</u>, which is your reasonable service."*
> **(Romans 12:1).**

A holy sacrifice is a sacrifice separated from the lusts of the flesh. Acceptable sacrifice is of a pure heart, independent from wrong motives which can be evil. This sacrifice is from the Spirit and can include using spiritual words which praise and magnify God in tongues.

Spiritual Sacrifice

The Lord is building us into spiritual priests, able to offer spiritual sacrifice. Instead of animal sacrifice, we offer the fruit offering of our lips to the Lord that is holy and spiritual.

> *"You also, like living stones, are being build into a spiritual house to be a holy priesthood, offering spiritual sacrifices acceptable to God through Jesus Christ."*
>
> **(1Peter 2:5 NIV).**

The Lord Jesus declared that true worshipers "shall" worship in Spirit and in truth. In Spirit means in the Holy Spirit (tongues). In truth means in the Word of God because the Word is truth. Worshiping in truth is in line with the Word of God.

> *"But the hour cometh, and now is, when the true worshippers shall worship the Father in spirit and in truth: for the Father seeketh such to worship him."*
>
> **(John 4:23).**

The Lord Jesus declared that true worshippers **"SHALL,"** worship in Spirit. The word "shall," was used to mean that at the time when the Holy Spirit has fully come, then shall worshipers worship in Spirit and in truth. As a spiritual priesthood, our sacrifice must always be in Spirit first then in truth. This is sacrifice, which is acceptable unto our God. The **"SHALL"** that the Lord declared is in effect now, because the Lord

Jesus is resurrected and reigning on high and the Holy Spirit has fully come to dwell in us and among us.

The Holy Spirit gives us spiritual words that are without spot or blemish. Spiritual words holy and worthy to use when sacrificing to the almighty God in Spirit. The Lord Jesus declared that the Holy Spirit is the Spirit of truth and He (the Spirit) will lead us into all truth. All truth means in every way of our spiritual walk, praising and worshiping included.

In Spirit and in Truth

Tongues helps us worship and praise the Lord in Spirit, as the apostle Paul boldly declared:

"For if I pray in an unknown tongues, my spirit prayeth, but my understanding is unfruitful."
(1 Corinthians 14:14).

Worshiping in Spirit always leads to worshipping in truth. It is worshiping in Spirit that aligns our hearts to worship in truth. The scripture tells us that the Spirit of God reminds us of all the things we need to know. He teaches us all truth. Even in worship, the Spirit of God directs us on how to pray in understanding so that it is in line with His truth.

"But the hour cometh, and now is, when the true worshippers shall worship the Father in spirit and in truth: for the Father seeketh such to worship him."
(John 4:23).

The scripture boldly declare that the Father is seeking for believers who worship Him in Spirit and in Truth **(John 4:24)**. This is because the Spirit leads us in all truth even as we worship.

Apostle Paul also ascribed to this principle of "in Spirit" first, then in truth. This is shown when he declared to the Corinthians church that he could sing in the Spirit and understanding as shown the scripture below:

> *"What is it then? I will pray with the spirit, and I will pray with understanding <u>also</u>: I will sing with the spirit and I will sing with understanding <u>also</u>. "*
>
> **(1 Corinthians 14:15).**

The word **"ALSO"** used in the above scripture gives the order in which this praying and singing must be done. Praying and singing in the Spirit is a prerequisite to praying and singing in understanding. Praising and worshipping in the Spirit sets the platform for praying and worshiping in understanding or in truth.

Praising and worshiping in tongues or in the Spirit is one of the sure ways of offering sacrifice that is spiritual, Holy and acceptable to God. This is because the flesh has no part in it. Walk and pray in the Spirit and you shall not gratify the desires of the flesh. Pray more in tongues and set yourself a platform to pray in truth, in line with God's perfect will!

11

Power of Tongues for Intercession

*"**So** I sought for a man among them who would make a wall, and stand in the gap before Me on behalf of the land, that I should not destroy it: but I found no one."*
(Ezekiel 22:30 NKJV).

The scripture above reveals to us a truth that's otherwise hidden for casual observers. It indicates that for God to intervene into a situation someone must stand in the gap and intercede. However, for one to intercede effectively, one must know what the will of God is concerning a particular situation.

In the scripture above, no one knew what the will of God was concerning the land. God was looking for someone who had knowledge of His will, so He could cause him to intercede. But He found none. The Lord and father of our Lord Jesus Christ by His mercy and grace is the One who causes us both to will and to do according to His good pleasure(Philippians 2:13). The Lord is the one who causes the intercessor to intercede. He is always on the look out for people with understanding who can discern what His will is for a particular situation.

Intercession without understanding the will of God is futile. This is because if you do not have insight into the mind of God concerning a particular situation, you can be doing one thing when the Lord desires something else. You can be building where the Lord wants to destroy. The will of God is not always in what seems fair or right to man. The Lord God knows the beginning from the end. He knows what best is to happen at any particular moment in time and delights in using us to achieve His purposes.

The Death and Resurrection of Lazarus

"When Jesus heard that, He said, "This sickness is not unto death, but for the glory of God, that the Son of God may be glorified through it."

(John 11:4 NKJV).

The passage of scripture above shows us the importance of understanding the will of God before interceding. If the Lord Jesus did not understand the purpose of God for the death of Lazarus, He could have gone and healed him of his sickness. The Lord Jesus could have simply said a word and Lazarus could have been healed. Nevertheless, the Lord Jesus understood what the will of God was. It was so that God could glorify Him as the resurrection and the life showing He had the power of life and death at His command **(John 11:25)**. Lord Jesus even told His disciples that Lazarus was merely sleeping when in fact he had died. *"These things said he: and after that he saith unto them, Our friend Lazarus sleepeth; <u>BUT I GO, THAT I MAY AWAKE HIM OUT OF SLEEP.</u> Then said his disciples, Lord, if he sleep, he shall do well. Howbeit Jesus spake of his death, but they thought that he had spoken of taking of rest in sleep. Then said Jesus unto them plainly, Lazarus is dead. " (John 11:11-14).*

The Lord Jesus wanted us to know and understand that whosoever is in Him, even if he dies he lives. Jesus knew that the Father wanted to glorify Him as the resurrection and the life. This is why He allowed Lazarus to die. He had plans to receive greater glory. God the Father wanted to show that Jesus could resurrect Lazarus and be glorified as the resurrection and the life. *"And I am glad for your sakes that I was not there, to the intent ye may believe; nevertheless let us go unto him. " (John 11:15).*

Jesus used this opportunity to reveal His Christhood to the disciples. He even delayed going to Lazarus' funeral for four days specifically because He wanted to defy Jewish belief. This belief held that for three days the spirit of the deceased hovers around the body making resurrection possible. Therefore, Jesus went there four days after the burial to resurrect Lazarus from the dead contrary to the Jewish belief.

"Then when Jesus came, he found that he had lain in the grave four days already. "

(John 11:17).

Tongues Show Us the Will of God

The Spirit who knows what the purpose of God is, prays for us and in us according to the will of God. The only sure way to intercede is to do so in the Spirit. Through praying in the Spirit, we are assured of praying in the will of God, because the Spirit knows and leads us in the will of God.

"And he that searcheth the hearts knoweth what is the mind of the Spirit, because he maketh intercession for the saints according to the will of God. "

(Romans 8:27).

The above scripture gives us a truth that is very important for everyone who intercedes in prayer. Knowing the mind of the Spirit helps us pray according to the will of God. The scripture tells us that the Spirit, who searches our hearts, also knows the mind of God and therefore can help us to intercede and will intercede for us according to the will of God.

"...for we know not what we should pray for as we ought: but the Spirit itself(Himself) maketh intercession for us with groanings which cannot be uttered. "

(Romans 8:26).

Many times, we find ourselves in desperate situations. Situations in which we do not exactly know what the will of God may be. Of course, we do know for certain that the will of God is found in the Word of God. However, there are times we feel we do not have any revelations concerning some particular situations. In such situations, the only sure way of praying is praying in tongues. This is because in tongues the Spirit of the Lord makes intercession for you and in you according to the will of God for your situation.

It is still advisable to pray more in tongues during your normal intercessary meetings. In the Spirit, you speak mysteries concerning your request, person or situation. The Spirit knows the mind of God and therefore speaks the will of God concerning that request and situation. Many are the times we need angels to work on our behalf in certain situations. However, if we do not ask Him to send them, they will not be able to intervene in our situation. Angels are ministering spirits called to serve those called to salvation **(Hebrews 1:14)**. In tongues, we speak the language of angels; even if it eludes our minds, in the Spirit we give instructions to the angels to battle on our behalf.

> *"Though I speak with the tongues of men and of angels... "*
>
> **(1 Corinthians 13:1).**

In the Spirit, we can pray the will of God for all saints. We all are at different growth levels and therefore cannot have the same requests and supplications. In tongues we can pray for all saints according to their requests and supplications. For it is the Spirit who understands the mind of God praying in us and we in Him. It is the Spirit who is all knowing and all sufficient for every saint praying and interceding for the saints through our spirits. The Spirit who lives in all saints searches the hearts of all saints and intercedes according to the desires of their hearts and the will of God. We have the ability to be relevant in every individual life by the power of praying in tongues. Praying in the Holy Ghost! "Kabashing!"

The Power of Tongues Beyond Limitations

We are not omnipresent, we are not all knowing. Therefore we cannot be as effective as we ought to be in our priestly duties of praying for all saints. We mostly cannot tell when our loved ones are in trouble and need our prayers. But the Holy Spirit can burden us with a mandate for prayer even before we know what it is concerning. The Spirit of God will direct our prayers in accordance with His will regardless of our emotional feelings at the time. Praise the Lord our reliance is upon Him and not in ourselves!

> *"Likewise the Spirit also helps our weakness for we do not know what we should pray for as we ought, but the Spirit Himself makes intercession for us with groanings which cannot be uttered."*
>
> **(Romans 8:26 NKJV).**

The word **"weakness,"** comes from a Greek word, **"ASTHENEIA"** which also means limitations. There are many times we are limited in our praying either by lack of knowledge, sickness, or strength. We sometimes are too tired to pray. Many times, we are not aware of

131

what is happening in places we are not. In the face of such limitations, praying in tongues helps us a great deal. For in the Spirit we deal with things that we are limited to naturally. Tongues give us the power to jump over our limitations and deal with things as and when we need to regardless of distance, time, and presence. We deal with spiritual realities before they manifest into the physical. Thereby, defying all the limitations of knowledge, distance, and any other natural limitations.

Speaking in tongues gives us the ability to change things in the realm of the spirit. We do not wrestle with flesh and blood but with spiritual wickedness in the high places. In tongues, we deal with the cause and not just the effects. In the spirit we deal with the controlling force. Tongues present us with the ability to pray in the will of God. The limitations that limit us from praying the right way, for the exact thing and the people in places we are not. Through praying in tongues all these limitations are eliminated. This is because tongues is not from our minds. It is only the Spirit of God in us who prays and works the will of God in us and for us. Glory to God!

Groaning the Power of Tongues for Resurrection

Tongues of groaning in the Spirit are a type of tongues of intercession. The Spirit prays for us and on our behalf in times of limitations through tongues of groaning. The Spirit prays for us and within us with groanings that are inexpressible in words. This is purely the Holy Spirit making intercession for us in situations where we are weak.

Power of Tongues for Intercession

> **"...but the Spirit Himself makes intercession for us with groanings which cannot be uttered."**
> **(Romans 8:28 NKJV).**

I remember in the year 2009, the Spirit of God brought me frequently into tongues of groaning. This time I was student with this leadership institution. Every time we had worship or prayer time, I would usually be groaning in the Spirit. Each time I groaned, I could feel like I was carrying or lifting a heavy load. My physical reactions were also of a person struggling with carrying a heavy load. However, one thing I noticed was that each time I got a relief from my groans, the presence of God would spontaneously increase in the room.

This happened several times without me realizing what was taking place. I realised that the Spirit was groaning in me more, but I did not pay attention to my bodily reactions. Until one day one of my leaders said, *"Do you know that you carry all of us into the deeper presence of God?"* He went on to explain that when I do my hands like I am carrying a heavy load in my groaning, I am actually carrying everyone along with me into the deeper presence of the Lord. This made a lot of sense to me because it could explain why I felt like I was carrying such a heavy load each time I was groaning.

Through my groaning, the Spirit could remove the limitations that inhibited the rest of the team from accessing the presence of God as they ought. He could use me as an available vessel to birth a deeper presence in the team. The Spirit uses the tool of groaning only in situations where death is present. It might be spiritual death, dullness of perception to understand the mysteries of God, or even actual physical death like in the story of Lazarus.

The story of Lazarus in **John 11** shows us how the Lord Jesus used the power of groaning in the Spirit to bring back Lazarus from the dead against all odds:

> **"...When Jesus therefore saw her weeping, and the Jews also weeping which came with her, he groaned in the spirit, and was troubled.**
> **(John 11:33 KJV).**

The above scripture meant that the Spirit groaned from within the Lord Jesus' body making intercession for Lazarus. The word **"groaning"** comes from a Greek word **"EMBRIMAOMAI"** which means *"to snort with anger"* or *"to straightly charge."* This means that the Holy Spirit moved with anger against the condition of Lazarus with groans. The process of groaning starts when the Holy Spirit is angry at a particular death condition and charges or snorts with anger and reviles against it. This is also known as holy or righteous anger. The scripture indicates that the Spirit continued charging against the condition of Lazarus until he was resurrected back to life. The Lord Jesus understood the power of groaning for resurrection life. He moved in the Spirit making intercession with groans continuously until the time the miracle was accomplished.

The scripture in John 11: 38 shows that the Lord Jesus continued groaning in the Spirit until the time when He was sure the work was done. The Lord then simply called Lazarus forth from the tomb because He knew that the resurrection work was already completed in the Spirit.

> ***"Then Jesus, again groaning in Himself, came to the tomb. It was a cave, and a stone lay against it."***
>
> **(John 11:38 NKJV).**

The tense used in the above scripture is present continuous. **"Groaning in himself,"** this shows us that the Lord Jesus groaned in Himself continuously all the way to the tomb. When He reached the tomb where Lazarus was buried, He thanked the Father for having heard Him when he groaned in the Spirit. ***"Then they took away the stone from the place where the dead was laid. And Jesus <u>lifted up his eyes, and said, Father, I thank thee that thou hast heard me.</u>"*** *(John 11:41)*. The Lord Jesus thanked the Father for hearing Him. There is nowhere in this passage of scripture where Jesus asked the Father to resurrect Lazarus. Glory to God!

> ***"And when he thus had spoken, he cried with a loud voice, Lazarus, come forth."***
>
> **(John 11:43).**

The Lord said, ***"Lazarus, come forth!"*** Death cannot keep you when Jesus is calling you to rise and live. In the Spirit, Jesus had already seen Lazarus raised.

12

Power of Tongues for Prophecy

*"**I** wish you all spoke with tongues, but even more that you prophesied; for he who prophesies is greater than he who speaks with tongues, UNLESS indeed he interprets, that the church may receive edification."*
(1 Corinthians 14: 5 NKJV).

The whole essence of the gift of prophecy is the benefit of edification to the church. The above opening scripture brings in a truth that is not plain to the casual observer. The scripture declares that when you interpret a tongue into a language understandable by the church to bring edification, then that tongue become a prophecy.

To understand best the role of prophecy in the church will help us appreciate the power of tongues for prophesying. The word edification comes from a Greek root word, which means to be *a house builder or to construct a concrete structure.* This then means that as a prophet prophesies to the church, he builds and constructs a spiritual concrete structure in the body of Christ. The word prophet means an *inspired man.* When a prophet prophesies by the inspiration of the Holy Spirit, he speaks what the Spirit gives and shows.

The word tongue as used in the above opening scripture comes from a Greek word **"GLOSSA."** Glossa means *"a language naturally unacquired or a language not naturally acquired."* Only the Holy Spirit can give this language supernaturally. Therefore, prophecy and tongues come from the same source which is the Holy Spirit. They both have the same function for edification. The only difference between the two is the languages used and the targeted recipients. The scripture commends us to pray and ask for interpretation if we speak in tongues to the church. This means that when we receive interpretation for the tongues spoken, we receive words divinely given by the Holy Spirit to communicate to the church for the purpose of edification. Words inspired by the Spirit of God, Words fit for edification to the church.

"Therefore let him who speaks in a tongue pray that he may interpret."

(1 Corinthians 14:13).

"If anyone speaks in a tongue, let there be two or at the most three, each in turn, and let one interpret."

(1 Corinthians 14:27).

Depth of Tongues for Prophecy

"How is it then, brethren? Whenever you come together, each of you has a psalm, has a teaching, has a tongue, has a <u>REVELATION</u>, has an <u>INTERPRETATION</u>, Let all things be done for <u>EDIFICATION</u>. "

(1 Corinthians 14:27).

The main essence of tongues is the benefit of edification. The above scripture brings in two vital ingredients to the tongues of prophecy to enhance edification to the individual and the church as a body. If you have a revelation and an interpretation of a tongue, let all be done for edification.

Revelation of Tongues:

Revelations of the mysteries spoken in tongues comes to your spirit as you speak in tongues. This happens as you begin to get insight and understanding of the things you are speaking in tongues. You will find that you understand scriptures which you never understood before. God imparts revelatory truths within you that previously eluded you. You open the scriptures only to confirm the things already revealed to your spirit. This is one of the basic ways in which revelation of tongues occurs as you pray.

Tongues present us with so much depth in the spiritual so that we can get as much revelation of God as our hearts desire from the Spirit.

"Which things also we speak, not in words which man's wisdom teaches, but which the Holy Spirit teaches, comparing spiritual things with spiritual things." (1 Corinthians 2:13 WEB). Through speaking in tongues, the Holy Spirit reveals to our spirits the deep things of God. The Spirit by tongues compares spiritual things of the depths of God with Spiritual things in our spirits and lives.

Every time God gives something to people, His delight is in people understanding and comprehending it so that they can get the maximum benefit. Revelation of tongues answers the "WHY?" question. It gives us the reason for the tongue spoken and shows the why that the tongue was given.

The book of Daniel 5 gives us the best example of revelation of tongues. This chapter gives an account of when God wrote on the wall in a tongue (Spiritual language). In this account are hidden examples of the revelation and the interpretation of tongues. The classic example of "why?" the tongue was given was written on the wall shown in the scripture below:

"And thou his son, o Belshazzar, has not humbled thine heart, though thou knewst all this; But has lifted up thyself against the Lord of heaven; and they have brought the vessels of his house before thee, and thou, and thy lords, thy wives, and thy concubines, have drunk wine in them; and thou hast praised the gods of Silver, and Gold, of brass, iron, wood, and stone, which see not, nor hear, nor know: and the God in whose hand thy breath is, and whose are all thy ways, hast not glorified:"

(Daniel 5:22-23).

The scripture above shows how Daniel gave the king the reason for the writing (tongue). He gave the King the revelation behind the writing. He gave him insight into the tongue written on the wall. He gave the King the reason <u>WHY</u> the Lord wrote on the wall.

Interpretation of Tongues:

Interpretation of tongues on the other hand gives us the meaning of a tongue spoken in a familiar language. This is merely translating the tongue into a language one can understand naturally. Interpretation of tongues translates the supernatural language into a natural language. Interpretation of tongues translates a tongue into a natural language that makes sense to the natural mind, like English, French, etc.

Interpretation of tongues answers the "<u>WHAT?</u>" question. It gives us the "what?" of the spiritual language into a natural language. The same book of Daniel 5 below, the Prophet Daniel translated the words written on the wall into a language the King could understand along with the meaning of the Lord's message behind the simple words. This answers the "what?" question as shown below:

> *"And this is the writing that was written, MENE; God hath numbered thy kingdom, and finished it.TEKEL; Thou art weighed in the balances, and art found wanting. PERES; Thy kingdom is divided, and given to the Medes and Persians. "*
>
> **(Daniel 5:25-27).**

The combination of the translation and revelation of tongues gives us an insight that is so complete in every aspect. It gives a deep and full understanding of the things of God. The Spirit of God using the tool of revelation and interpretation gives us the deep things of God.

13

The Power of Tongues in Familiar Languages

"So likewise you, unless you utter by the tongue words easy to understand, how will it be known what is spoken? For you will be speaking into the air."

(1 Corinthians 14:9).

The scripture above declares that it is possible to speak in a tongue words easy to understand naturally. *"Unless you utter by the tongues or in a tongue words easy to understand,"* shows that it is possible to speak in a tongue words in a natural, earthly language. This means that the Holy Spirit can give you a natural language supernaturally. This means you would speak in tongues in a language familiar to many; like English, French, and Hebrew etc.

The word tongue as used in the opening scripture above comes from a Greek word **"GLOSSA"** which means a language that cannot be acquired through learning. This means that no one can naturally learn the words referred to as *"easy to understand"* in the above scripture. The Holy Spirit gives these words. Any language that comes by learning in a logical way is naturally acquired. It is not glossa and does not come from the Holy Spirit. It is but just a dialect.

Tongues in familiar languages can occur when the person the Lord wants to use does not have understanding or any knowledge of that particular language. In such cases, the Spirit gives utterance through the gift of tongues in a familiar language in order to communicate His will and achieve all that He desires. Such gifts of tongues eliminate language barriers which would otherwise inhibit the efficacy of conveying God's intended message. Believers should not be surprised at this special gift of tongues because the Spirit knows everything and that includes all languages, either heavenly or earthly. He is the one who gave the apostles all the different languages they used to minister to the diversity of people in Jerusalem on the day of Pentecost. *"And there appeared unto them cloven tongues like as of fire, and it sat upon each of them. And they were all filled with the Holy Ghost, and began to speak with other tongues, as the Spirit gave them utterance."* *(Acts 2:3-4)* The Holy Spirit of God gives these languages supernaturally for specific functions. They can be given at any time and in any natural language.

You do not have to learn these languages naturally but the Spirit of God through His divine power and ability gives us these languages for the purposes of the Kingdom. After the prophetic word is given, the speaker may or may not retain fluency and understanding in that language as the Lord so chooses.

Tongues Break Language Barriers

The power of tongues in familiar languages breaks the barriers of communication. It makes it possible to communicate with everyone in his or her own languages. The scriptures below show that the multitudes of people were confused because they all came from different parts of the world and knowingly spoke with many different languages, yet all heard the disciples speak to them in their own native tongues. This is the account of Pentecost when the Holy Spirit descended from on high and distributed gifts of tongues to the apostles, the disciples of our Lord Jesus.

> *"And when this sound occurred, the multitudes came together, and were confused, because everyone heard them speak in his own language."*
>
> **(Acts 2:6 NKJV).**

> *"And how is it that we hear, each in our own language in which we were born?"*
>
> **(Acts 2:8 NKJV).**

In the book of Genesis 11, there is an account of a story about man's desire to build themselves a city and a tower for the wrong reasons. For reasons that were contrary to the plan of God.

"And they said, Go to, let us build us a City and a tower; whose top may reach unto heaven; and let us make us a name, lest we be scattered abroad."
(Genesis 11:4).

Men came together and devised a plan to build a city and a tower so that they could be all in one place. They had wanted to glorify themselves rather than the Lord through the works of their hands. They did not want to spread out and populate the whole earth contrary to the plan of the Creator. For this reason, God the Father in His sovereign power divided them by changing their languages that they may not communicate. Eventually they all separated from one another and scattered in all directions due to language barriers.

Due to man's disobedience, God changed the languages of the peoples of the earth to divide and scatter them. Now in order to gather the people to Himself in Christ, He graciously gave us the power to speak many languages by the utterance given by the Holy Spirit through tongues in familiar languages. These tongues are for the work of bringing back the people to God. The work of reconciling the world to God.

Power to Minister to All Peoples

It is a known fact, recorded in the Bible and other books of history that the disciples of the Lord Jesus were Jews. Many, if not all came from the region of Galilee and mainly spoke the Galilean native dialect. Most of the disciples were not educated in this worldly education. However, on Pentecost they spoke in many languages they did not naturally know. The Holy Spirit gave them these utterances to minister to the broad spectrum of people that were present on that day. *"Then they were all amazed and marvelled, saying to one another, "Look, are not all these who speak Galileans?"*

(Acts 2:7).

"Cretans and Arabs—we hear them speaking in our own tongues the wonderful works of God."

(Acts 2:11 NKJV).

Through the power of tongues in familiar languages, the simple disciples of Jesus marvelled many people. The uneducated disciples all of the sudden began to speak the wonderful works of God in languages previously foreign to them. The Holy Spirit accomplished this through them for the purposes of communicating the wonderful works of God to people of different languages. This still remains a wonder to many and is only accomplished by the divine work of the Holy Spirit. As a result of this supernatural ability, many believers were added to the number of the followers of Christ. The scriptures record that about three thousand souls were added to the church. This tool of tongues in familiar languages is still at work today. All we need to do is ask for the gift from the giver of gifts who is the Holy Spirit. This gift should be for the purposes of accomplishing more in the area of adding more souls to the church. This tongue is for the purposes of evangelising the world.

"Then those who gladly received his word were baptized. There were added that day about three thousand souls."

(Act 2:41WEB).

146

The Power of Tongues in Familiar Languages

Ask for the gift of tongues in familiar languages and operate supernaturally in natural languages. Remember this is for the purposes of expanding the Kingdom of God. The Spirit gives gifts for His service and not for individual prestige. To the Glory to God!

14

Creative Abilities of Speaking in Tongues

"When the Day of Pentecost had fully come, they were all in one accord in one place. And suddenly there came a sound from heaven, as of a rushing mighty wind, and it filled the whole house where they were sitting. Then there appeared to them <u>divided tongues, as of fire, and one sat upon each of them.</u> And they were all filled with the Holy Spirit and began to speak with other tongues, as the Spirit gave them utterance. "

(Acts 2:1-4 NKJV).

On the day the Holy Spirit finally came to the world, He came with the gift of tongues. The Spirit came with divided cloven tongues that He distributed among all the disciples. The gift of tongues that came with the Holy Spirit on the day of Pentecost brought us the ability to

148

create. The Spirit of God always comes with creative abilities. **(Psalms 104:30).** This ability to create from the Holy Spirit comes through the gift of tongues. God the creator in Genesis chapter 1 created the heavens and the earth with words in the presence of the Holy Spirit.

> *"…And the Spirit of God moved upon the face of the waters. And God said, Let there be light: and there was light."*
>
> **(Genesis 1:2-3).**

Tongues are spiritual words that come from the Holy Spirit. The gift of tongues and the presence of the Holy Spirit form a perfect partnership for creation. When the Spirit fully came as recorded in the above opening scripture He came with His own utterance to give us this ability to create. Creation is making something from nothing using words latent with the awesome power of God.

The Holy Spirit and the Word of God are the two elements that are never absent during creation. Creation is making something out of nothing using Words in the presence of the Holy Spirit. The coming of the Holy Spirit came with the gift of tongues to give us the ability to create. The ability to create is packaged in the utterance given by the Holy Spirit, which are tongues. The Holy Spirit avails us with the abilities that are only present in the Godhead. These abilities are only accessible to those who have divinity dwelling in them.

> *"…; but you know Him, for He dwells with you and will be <u>IN YOU</u>."*
>
> **(Luke 14:17 NKJV).**

The indwelling of the Holy Spirit in you means divinity dwells in you. This gives you the creative abilities of the Godhead. The indwelling of the Holy Spirit in you meets the requirements for creation to take place in you and through you. You have both the Word and the presence of the Holy Spirit dwelling in you. All you need to do is to speak those words of the Spirit more (brooding), until you get charged enough to create God's ideal world with your own words in understanding (Rhema word in you).

The Power in You to Create

"But you shall receive power (Dunamis) when the Holy Spirit has come upon you. "
(Acts 1:8 NKJV).

"...but tarry in the city of Jerusalem until you are endued with power (Dunamis) from on high. "
(Luke 24:49 NKJV).

The word dunamis also means the divine ability to cause change, the ability to do the miraculous. This also means the ability to create. When the Spirit of the Lord comes, He comes with the ability to create. This ability is found in the language of tongues and the anointing. The "power" as promised in the above scripture is all we need to cause effective changes in our lives.

This power is activated through speaking in tongues. Therefore speaking in tongues in an increasing measure along with a pure heart after God is all we need to create a desired future. The power of the Spirit to create is enhanced through the tool of speaking in tongues. He who speaks in tongues is building in himself a spiritual giant who operates in the most Holy faith. The most Holy faith is a level where creation in the Spirit is a normal operation.

The Way to Create

Prayer is important. If you really want to bring God into your situation, you have to pray. When you pray in the Spirit, something happens to you. Many people do not know how and why they should pray in the Spirit.

Every time you want an idea, you will get it in prayer. It is during the time of prayer that your spiritual eyes are open and you begin to see into spiritual realities. Then God will communicate with you through your creative spirit and something will come through. God will always give ideas in prayer. This is key to accessing that creative insight He has available to us. An idea from God is all you need. With that idea you can change the world as you know it.

You must therefore, spend time praying in the Spirit until the visions come to your spirit. You must continue meditating on the idea you got while praying in the Spirit until you can speak the word that will bring it to pass. When you speak the word upon that idea you received in your spirit, it becomes a reality in the spirit realm. It is the ideas that come to you while you are praying in the Spirit that will bring your vision into the physical realm. If you meditate on these ideas long enough, until you are fully persuaded, they will become real to you and your dreams will materialize.

Do you want to achieve your goals? Then make up your mind! Through praying in the spirit, you can effectively change your future. You can create a future for yourself that you have always dreamed of living. Do not just complain about the status quo, but always engage the ministry of praying in the Spirit (praying in tongues) to tap into new ideas to birth new realities. Meditate on the ideas acquired in prayer and speak words of life, words inspired by the Holy Spirit.

By praying in the Spirit, you charge your spirit and prepare yourself to be aligned with God's thoughts. At this particular time, it is more appropriate to speak words that can create a future you desire while the Spirit of the Lord is still present.

Dr. Oral Roberts once said that after sowing a seed, he would speak in tongues or pray in the Spirit until he gets ideas from the Lord. Then he could write down the ideas and follow them through until he created the desired harvest. Praying in the Spirit prepares the ground for the creative spirit of man.

15

Power of Tongues in the Life of Apostle Paul

The life and ministry of apostle Paul serves as an example of how the ministry of speaking in tongues works. It gives us a brief summary into the power of speaking in tongues for your life and ministry. Apostle Paul received the same salvation as all the other apostles. He was one of the apostles, who did not share in the earthly ministry of our Lord Jesus. He only became a believer after he encountered the Lord Jesus on the road to Damascus.

The Apostle Paul received the same Holy Spirit as the other apostles did yet he excelled more in ministry. One of the secrets for Paul's success in ministry was the power of speaking in tongues. Paul is the apostle who received the revelations about tongues. He understood the mysteries of tongues more and got many revelations as a result.

Spoke in Tongues More

"I thank my God I speak with tongues more than you all; ..."
(1 Corinthians 14:18 NKJV).

Apostle Paul here in the scripture above boasted that he spoke more in tongues than they all did. He must have discovered the power released in tongues for him to speak with tongues more than everyone in Corinth did. Paul must have also spoken more in tongues than the other apostles did considering the amount of revelations he reviewed about tongues. He said in privacy he could speak thousands of words in tongues but in the church, he would rather speak five words in understanding.

"Yet in the church I would rather speak five words with my understanding, that I may teach others also, than ten thousand words in a tongue."
(1 Corinthians 14:19 NKJV).

By this, Paul indicated that he had a good understanding of the truth that tongues brings edification. He therefore spoke more in tongues in privacy to edify himself. The apostle understood that by speaking in tongues he spoke mysteries with God and received from the Spirit the wisdom he needed for his daily life.

Grace for Ministry

"For I am the least of the apostles, who am not worthy to be called an apostle, because I persecuted the church of God."
                    (1 Corinthians 15:9 NKJV).

Apostle Paul here in the scripture above said he was not worthy to be counted among the apostles because he had formerly persecuted the church. However, after his encounter with the Lord, Paul worked more abundantly than all the other apostles. He experienced more of the Lord than all and had more grace for ministry. He wrote more than half of the books in the New Testament and laboured more for the sake of the gospel than all others.

"...But I laboured more abundantly than they all, yet not I, but the grace of God which was me."
                    (1 Corinthians 15:10 NKJV).

How did the least become the best? What made him work with such grace that he surpassed all the apostles the Lord Jesus himself trained? I believe one of the reasons apostle Paul was able to go the extra mile was because he understood the fight he was fighting. He knew he was fighting the fight of faith. *"I have fought a good fight, I have finished my course, I have kept the faith."* *(2 Timothy 4:7)* To win this fight of faith one needs to build their faith to the most holy faith. This is done through praying in the Holy Ghost. *"But ye, beloved, building up yourselves on your most holy faith, praying in the Holy Ghost."* *(Jude 1:20).*

Apostle Paul learned the secret of speaking in tongues to grow in grace and build his faith to the most Holy Faith.

Deeper Revelations

"And lest I should be exalted above measure by the abundance of the revelations... "
(2 Corinthians 12: 7 NKJV).

The scripture says that apostle Paul had surprisingly great revelations. He was receiving abundant revelations because his spirit was always in tune with the Holy Spirit. He tuned his spirit to the Lord by speaking in tongues consistently. He got many revelations through speaking in tongues; in tongues we speak mysteries that when unveiled become revelations. The more tongues he spoke the more revelations he got because the Holy Spirit who is the teacher and the giver of revelations became one with his spirit.

"But now, brethren, if I come to you speaking with tongues, what shall I profit you unless I speak to you either by <u>revelation</u>…"
(1 Corinthians 14:6 NKJV).

Apostle Paul received many truths through divine revelations. He would speak in tongues, receive revelations in his spirit, and then teach the church the things he received from the Spirit. *"But I certify you, brethren, that the gospel which was preached of me is not after man. For I neither received it of man, neither was I taught it, but by the revelation of Jesus Christ."* *(Galatians 1:11-12)*

"For I have received of the Lord that which also I delivered unto you, ... "
(1Corinthians 11:23).

Apostle Simon Peter once said that the writings and the wisdom God gave to Paul was difficult to comprehend. Other apostles also knew that Paul had a rich depth of revelation. He got these revelations from the Spirit of God through speaking in tongues. *"Now we have received, not the spirit of the world, but the spirit which is of God; that we might know the things that are freely given to us of God. Which things also we speak, not in the words which man's wisdom teacheth, but which the Holy Ghost teacheth; comparing spiritual things with spiritual. " (1Corinthians 2:12-13).*

The scripture declares that the Spirit who searches the deep things of God taught Paul that which God has freely given us. By speaking in tongues more, his spirit was fine tuned with the Holy Spirit, giving him access to the deeper things of God. This enabled Paul to comprehend things which had eluded all others. He had such a wealth of revelations concerning God and His son Jesus Christ that he even wrote more than half of the New Testament.

"And consider that the longsuffering of our Lord is salvation—as also our beloved brother Paul, according to the wisdom given to him, has written to you, as also in all his epistles, speaking in them of these things, in which are hard to understand, which untaught and unstable people twist to their own destruction, as they do also the rest of the scriptures. "
(2 Peter 3:15-16 NKJV).

157

These revelations were so deep that people twisted their minds in order to understand them. Apostle Paul was even mistaken for a god because of the vastness of his knowledge and miraculous works. The revelations Paul received were sometimes truly out of this world. He said he went to the third heaven where he heard things he could not mention; the things he heard were not earthly but heavenly. Paul was a constant and consistent tongue talker which yielded great power in his life and ministry to the glory of God!

Peculiar Anointing

In the scripture, it is recorded that apostle Paul worked strange miracles. If the scriptures could call Paul's miracles special then they must have been different from the other miracles the other apostles performed.

"And God wrought special miracles by the hands of Paul: So that from his body were brought unto the sick handkerchiefs or aprons, and the diseases departed from them, and the evil spirits went out of them."

(Acts 19:11-12).

He operated at a senior level in the Spirit such that even handkerchiefs and aprons that touched his body would carry the anointing power to heal the sick and drive out evil spirits. Paul was a master harvester. He won more souls in stadium style meetings, planted more churches, disciple more people, and became the most read author and apostle to the present day. He brought a holy revolution to both the church and the Roman Empire. Apostle Paul had the faith and unabashed boldness to present the Gospel to the ruling powers of his day. He converted the ruler of Cyprus, and almost converted Governor Felix while in chains. On several occasions he was beaten to the point of death, was imprisoned, even shipwrecked yet the Lord rescued him from them all so that could continue his work for Him.

The Order He Prayed

The apostle Paul followed a certain order when praying. He prayed in the same way prophesied by the Lord Jesus as recorded in the book of John 4:23. The Lord Jesus declared that true worshipers shall worship in SPIRIT and in TRUTH. In Spirit, is in the Holy Spirit or in tongues; in truth is in understanding but in line with the word of God.

> *"But the hour is coming, and now is, when the true worshipers will worship the father in Spirit and truth; for the father is seeking such to worship."*
>
> **(John 4:23 NKJV).**

> *"God is Spirit, and those who worship Him must worship in Spirit and truth."*
>
> **(John 4:24 NKJV).**

The Lord is Spirit and he who prays must pray to Him in Spirit. Paul understood the key to a powerful prayer life. To be effective, one must pray in Spirit and then in Truth because the Lord is Spirit. He understood that the Spirit leads us into all truth. Therefore, prayers must be of the Spirit so that the Spirit can lead us into all truth.

The apostle Paul prayed in the same order of **"in Spirit and in truth."** Many believers in the modern church neglect to heed this when they pray. They pray in predominately in understanding and then cap off their prayers with a few tongues before saying amen. If only they understood what the Holy Spirit can do when you tap into Him through praying in tongues!

> *"What is the conclusion then? I will pray with the spirit, and I will <u>also</u> pray with understanding..."*
> **(1 Corinthian14: 15 NKJV).**

Apostle Paul used the word "ALSO" to mean that, the order of praying is very important for the effectiveness of your prayers. Praying in the spirit (in tongues) aligns your spirit and mind to the will of God. It helps you pray in the will of God. It helps you speak mysteries in the Spirit that is truth.

16

Discovering Tongues
(Testimonies)

$\mathcal{T}$hursday, October 22nd 2009, I ministered on the Power of the Holy Spirit at the Disciples of God Program. The Disciples of God was a discipleship program we had among the young people. I ministered on the Power of the Holy Spirit and there was such a strong presence of the anointing of the Holy Spirit that there were many manifestations of His power.

People who never believed in the power of the Holy Spirit and those who thought that tongues were for a selected group of people were proven wrong by the tangible working of the Holy Spirit. The Holy Spirit moved in the meeting so strongly that a good number of people were baptised in the Spirit and spoke in tongues that very evening. Many others were ignited with a new and deeper awakening in the Spirit. Still more were refilled with the Holy Spirit and spoke in new and different kinds of tongues, to the Glory of the Most High!

One remarkable experience was an encounter with a young girl from Jeffery's Bay. She was only eleven years of age and she came to ask me to pray for her family. She was crying saying that she wants God to save her family. She even said that she was willing to die for her family to be saved. That was so surprising to me especially coming from an eleven year old. I prayed for her, asking God for grace for her family. When she went home that day, she jumped on her mother, laying hands on her and praying in tongues.

The presence of the Holy Ghost was so strong upon her that everyone present regardless of age or race received of the Spirit of God. The second girl of about sixteen years of age was baptised in the Spirit during the meeting. This girl spoke in other tongues from the time of the meeting, from 5pm to 6am the following morning. The girl was so overwhelmed by the power of the Holy Ghost that we had to take her home "drunk in the Spirit" and still speaking in tongues. The ordeal continued until the following morning and days thereafter to the praise of His Glory!

Then there was another girl who was possessed by demons. This girl was so aggressive and violent that she had to be taken some place for prayer. The people prayed for her for some time but her condition did not change. It was then that they called me to her. When I entered the room, the girl immediately attacked me, but could not harm me. I looked at her and saw the rage in her eyes. I then brought her down and rebuked the demon out her. When the girl was released from the demonic force and came to her senses, she immediately mentioned my name. I asked her to tell me more about her family and she told me how she hated her Dad for neglecting her and her siblings. I counselled her and told her to forgive her Dad for everything he had done and for the father he was not. She agreed to forgive her father so I asked her to write down whatever she wanted to tell her father.

After the whole process, I prayed for her and she was baptised in the Spirit. When she went out to the main hall, she immediately started speaking in other tongues. She spoke in tongues non-stop from about 6:00 pm to the following morning. We took her home speaking in other tongues. I remember her mother thinking when we brought her home that she was possessed by demons. How surprised she was to find that she was peaceful and of sound mind yet speaking in tongues uncontrollably. She was overwhelmed by the presence of the Holy Spirit and His healing work within her.

I got a few testimonies from the people who attended the meeting to give an account of their experiences on that night. Here are some of the testimonies I received:

"Last night I experienced God like I never had before. I was going through an emotional time in my life; my mum got sick this time of the year and died three years ago. It's hard for me to move on because I never mourned for her, and now my emotions are high. My sister and I have no one to talk to now and she lives in Johannesburg so we do not have a chance to talk that much. My guardians have been fighting over me and it hurts. Most of the time when my uncle is drunk he says hurtful things to me and my dad abandoned me.

However, yesterday I felt God's Spirit in me, I was overwhelmed by his love. He showed me a side of myself that I haven't seen before. It felt like a burden was lifted off my shoulders and He was telling me, everything is going to be okay. I was a bit scared and I just cried, I felt a healing in me. His light was shining in my heart. I've never experienced such healing power, last night I got a sign from God that everything will be okay, and He's always there for me."

Palesa - Cradock, South Africa.

"My understanding of the gifts of tongues was very limited up until a few years ago. I grew up going in a southern Baptized Church in Eugene, Oregan, USA. I do not remember receiving any teaching on the gifts of the Holy Spirit; any questions I asked regarding such passages of scripture were swept aside with an explanation to the effect that tongues and other miracles are not in effect today. Those answers left me wondering about the hunger I felt for deep thing of God based on the prophesies and Jesus' promises in scripture about the Holy Spirit.

Last year, around September 2008, I received the gift of tongues. I was at a weekly gathering of a house church I'd been attending in San Diego California since the start of the year. We were seeking God in prayer and worship and I felt a deep longing to encounter him in a new way. At some point as I was praying, I felt a sensation in my throat, as though something was bubbling up wanting to come out of my mouth. I opened my mouth and uttered a few words in a language I didn't know. I went into the other room to test out these new words. I'm ashamed to say I didn't believe what was happening at first, to actually be speaking in tongues.

I felt more like a baby learning to speak than what I imagined tongues to be based on my knowledge of the Day of Pentecost in Acts 2. I tested out my new gifts a few times after that night, but sadly left it dormant for about six months. In March 2009, I was a student in a training program for simple church planters in Cape Town, South Africa. We were blessed by a week of teachings on the Holy Spirit by a powerful man of God from Scotland. I made an appointment to speak with him towards the end of the week, to ask about my questioned gift of tongues. He prayed for me to receive, and as he prayed, I began to speak those same few words I'd received months ago in San Diego. He explained to me that the Holy Spirit manifests his gifts in different ways and I should not be confused that I received only a few words in a seemingly unremarkable manner. He encouraged me to practice my new tongue and in doing so I would grow in confidence and intimacy with the gift giver himself. I did that and was amazed at the impact on my prayer life. When I was at loss for words when interceding, I would allow the Spirit to take over. When I worshiped, I would speak in tongues to express the deep feelings I felt English inadequate to articulate. When having quiet time with the Lord, I would speak to Him in tongues to enjoy intimacy of sharing words that even I could not understand but experience the meaning in my spirit.

My most powerful experience with tongues came just at the end of last week. On Thursday 22nd October 2009, we were holding a meeting with a group of youths to teach them and provide an opportunity for them to encounter the Holy Spirit, who had already been moving mightily among them. As the Holy Spirit met us in that time, many demons began to manifest in the youth. As I prayed for deliverance of one girl, in particular I felt compelled to pray in tongues as I held my hands on her head. Her eyes rolled around in their socket and she shrunk under my hands. I was amazed at the power of the Heavenly language in doing battle with the forces of darkness.

Another friend who was praying for the same girl with me, later testified that when I prayed in tongues he heard what sounded like many angels speaking, not in human voices. It has been an exciting journey the past year of learning to use the gifts God has given me. I am grateful He has blessed me with tongues. He allowed me to participate is such mighty moves of the Dear Holy Spirit. I still have much to learn, but I trust through studying of the scriptures and continuing to be open to the leading and teaching of the Holy Spirit I will walk in greater confidence and power with the Lord. He is faithful to His promise that when we seek Him with our whole hearts we will find Him."

Elizabeth Jones - Oregan, USA.

"When the Holy Spirit fell on me, I could not stand on my feet. The more I wanted to stand, the more I fell to the ground. While on the ground I started speaking in tongues. It was my very first time to speak in tongues. In my church we don't speak in tongues! No one teaches about speaking in tongues. It was a new thing in my life. I go to the Anglican Church and no one teaches about tongues.

My life has changed ever since that Thursday. I am more hungry and thirsty for God. My perception of Christianity has changed. I think differently and see things differently. Thank you Father for the gift of the Holy Spirit."

Lifa Jolobe - Grahamstown, South Africa.

"I had a vision that angels got in and out of heaven when the Holy Spirit showed up and rested on people. I was left out, but my prayer to God was do not pass me by, because I was guarding on the door that no one would run away or any one that was demon possessed would escape. Therefore, after my short prayer, the Spirit of God fell on me and showed me the power and splendour of God Himself.

I must say what I saw with my own eyes; I saw a big light shine when it was dark in the room. I couldn't believe it but then it appeared again. I was rebaptised in the Spirit and spoke in new and different tongues. I felt God around me. I just wanted to be in His presence. My eyes have seen the lightness of God and have seen how angels look like because of the Holy Spirit."

Moses Mwaula - Lusaka, Zambia.

"I believe in tongues, I was baptised in the Holy Spirit and began to speak in other tongues in January 2007. However, this did not really mean much to me until this year (2009) when I started experiencing different kinds of tongues and my spiritual life was never the same.

Many times when I am in the presence of God, I find myself in other tongues and the Holy Spirit manifesting in me with groans that words cannot express. I believe it is our birthright as believers to have the Holy Spirit and experience the gifts of tongues. The secret is in desiring the gifts of the Spirit, the more you desire the more you get. Blessings!"

Valentine Chirume - Zimbabwe.

Receiving the Holy Spirit

I believe you've been blessed by this edition and I trust that you've leant more about the mysteries of the language of angels- speaking in tongues. If you are already baptised in the Holy Ghost I pray that this has enlightened you to the greater truths about the gift you received. And if you have not yet received the baptism of the Holy Ghost I invite you to receive the baptism by going through this prayer with me as follows:

O Lord God, I come to You in the name of Jesus Christ. Your word says, "These signs shall follow them that believe; in my name... they shall speak with new tongues." (Mark 16:17)

I believe that Jesus Christ is the son of God. I believe that He came to die for my old nature so that He can give me a new nature. I believe that the Holy Spirit is my inheritance in my new nature. I believe in the baptism of the Holy Spirit with the evidence of speaking in tongues.

In the Name of Jesus Christ, I believe and therefore I receive the Holy Spirit. I receive the baptism of the Holy Spirit with the evidence of speaking in tongues. I believe and therefore I receive the baptism of the Holy Ghost In the Name of Jesus Christ. I thank you Lord for the infilling of the Holy Ghost in me. I have the Holy Ghost in me and I pray in tongues in the Holy Ghost In Jesus' Name Amen!

Start praising the Lord from this moment and speaking in tongues. Hallelujah!

END NOTES

* **Page 52 *"RAPHAH"***
  from the 07503 – Strong's Hebrew Dictionary

* **Page 52 *"YADA"* Also Page 94**
  from the 03045 – Strong's Hebrew Dictionary

* **Page 79 *"MEGALUNO"***
  from the 3170 – Strong's Greek Dictionary

* **Page 81 *"PROPHETEUO"***
  from the 4395 – Strong's Greek Dictionary

* **Page 110 *"OIKODOMEO"* for Edification**
  from the 3618 – Strong's Greek Dictionary

* **Page 115 *"EXOUSIA"* for Power**
  from the 1849 – Strong's Greek Dictionary

* **Page 116 *"DUNAMIS"* for Power. Also Page 58**
  from the 1411 – Strong's Greek Dictionary

* **Page 118 *"GINOSKO"* for Know**
  from the 1097 – Strong's Greek Dictionary

* **Page 118 *"GNOSIS"* for Knowledge**
  from the 1108 – Strong's Greek Dictionary

* **Page 119 *"EPOIKODOMEO"* for Building up. Also Page 65**
  from the 2026 – Strong's Greek Dictionary

* **Page 131 *"ASTHENEIA"* for Weakness**
  from the 2026 – Strong's Greek Dictionary

* **Page 134 *"EMBRIMAOMAI"***
  from the 1690 – Strong's Greek Dictionary

* **Page 137 *"GLOSSA."* Also Page 142**
  from the 1100 – Strong's Greek Dictionary

ABOUT THE AUTHOR

I was born in a Christian family with my father having a prominent Godly influence over my life. I grew up going to Sunday school and keenly attending church programs. My father was an elder in Reformed church in Zambia.

It was in 1997 when I was 14 years old that I received the Lordship of Christ in my life. It happened at a teen fellowship called Junior Fellowship. At one meeting when there was a teaching about how Jesus paid the price for our sins and that in Him alone can man have salvation. I responded to the altar call and gave my life to Jesus, and after the regeneration of my inner man, I felt a sensation like electricity pass through my body and the presence of God enveloped my whole being.

From that very moment, I found fulfilment replacing every emptiness in my life and everything felt so new to me. The church program became more than just a program. It was full of life now. My entire being was transformed as I continued to fellowship and study the Word of God. I grew in the knowledge of Christ since then, and have experienced more of the Holy Spirit. From the year 2003 to date, I have been teaching the Word of God and have experienced the love and the faithfulness of God in confirming His Word with signs and wonders.

I have also developed some consultancy skills overtime due to my previous occupation working in investment banking and accountancy, and teaching on the personality profile at the Leadership Experience (LXP). I have also been teaching the oracles of God through preaching, discipleship, having conferences, and visiting schools for ministry. I pioneered a ministry in Zambia called Christ Ambassadors Outreach Team, a youth ministry that is still vibrant today in fulfilling the great commission.

I, Musa, am married to Hope and the Lord has blessed us with two children Mariska and Joash. We currently reside in South Africa, Eastern Cape Province, in a town called Jeffrey's bay, forty-five minutes drive east of Port Elizabeth, teaching the gospel of the kingdom at an organization called LXP-(The leadership experience). A Leadership Institution aimed at training native African Leaders and serving as an associate preacher and teacher at Ithemba Family Church in Jeffreys Bay South Africa.

Inviting Musa to Your Area

Musa may be available to speak at your church, conference or crusade. Please contact us with your details of your ministry and invitation. You must please give information pertaining to the nature of the program. Musa and his team will pray over your invitation and respond to you as soon as possible.

Contact us at

Musa George Mwanza
P.O Box 1015
Jeffery's Bay 6330,
Eastern Cape
South Africa.

E-mail: musagmwanza@gmail.com
Face book: Musa Mwanza
Blog: musageorge2020.wordpress.com